The Secrets to Swift Achievement

... ...

Unlock The Keys to Succeed Faster

Jason M. Traver

Copyright: © 2024 Jason M. Traver.

All rights reserved. No part of this book may be reproduced, distributed, or transmitted in any form or by any means, including photocopying, recording, or other electronic or mechanical methods, without the prior written permission of the publisher, except in the case of brief quotations embodied in critical reviews and certain other noncommercial uses permitted by copyright law.

Disclaimer Notice

The information provided in *The Secrets to Swift Achievement: Unlock The Keys to Succeed Faster* is for general informational and educational purposes only. While every effort has been made to ensure the accuracy and effectiveness of the content, the author and publisher make no guarantees or warranties, either express or implied, regarding the completeness, accuracy, or applicability of the information presented.

The strategies, tips, and techniques shared are based on personal experiences and research and may not be suitable for everyone. Success, growth, and achievement vary greatly depending on individual effort, circumstances, and other external factors. Therefore, results are not guaranteed, and readers are advised to use their discretion and seek professional guidance where necessary.

The author and publisher are not responsible for any losses, damages, or adverse effects that may arise from following the advice or recommendations in this book. By reading and applying the content, you acknowledge that you are doing so at your own risk and that success is ultimately dependent on your own actions.

For legal, financial, or professional advice, please consult a qualified professional.

Table of Content

Introduction	4
Part 1	9
Setting the Foundation	9
Chapter 1	16
Defining Success	16
Success from Various Angles	16
The Definition of Personal Success is Crucial	20
Goal-setting by beliefs and ambitions	25
Chapter 2	30
The Psychology of Achievement	30
Mindset and Belief Systems	30
Self-Efficacy and Confidence	37
Overcoming Limiting Beliefs	48
Part 2	57
Goal Setting and Planning	57
Chapter 3	58
Setting Smart Goals	58
Specificity, Measurability, Achievability, Relevance, Time-bound	58
Creating Goals That Work	64

Dividing Objective Into Doable Stages	68
Chapter 4	**71**
Creating Action Plans	71
Setting Task Priorities	72
Time-Management Techniques	85
Part 3	**106**
Productivity and Time Management	106
Chapter 5	**107**
Maximizing Productivity	107
Determining Peak Productive Times	108
Eliminating Distraction	112
Techniques of Focus and Concentration	116
Chapter 6	**126**
Time Management Skills	126
Having Limits and Refusing Requests	126
Making Use of Technological Tools to Manage Time	133
Part 4	**141**
Overcoming Challenges	141
Chapter 7	**142**
Building Resilience	142
Coping Mechanisms for Failures and Setbacks	146
Developing a Growth Mindset	156

Seeking for Assistance and Resources	165
Chapter 8	169
Embracing Change	169
Adapting to change	170
Converting Obstacles Into Chances	181
Flexibility and Agility in Decision Making	
188	
Chapter 9	192
Staying Motivated	192
Identifying Intrinsic Motivation	195
Acknowledging Advancement And	
Commemorating Successes	202
Part 5	205
Sustainability and Long-Term Success	205
Chapter 10	206
Sustainable Habits	206
Developing Routines and Rituals	206
Making Wellbeing and Self-care a Priority	
210	
Conclusion	219

Introduction

People who write down their goals are likely to achieve and improve their lives. They have a better chance of accomplishing their goals than those who keep their dreams in their heads. Have you written your goals down? Let's read a true story about a man called Alfred.

Alfred had always been an average man with a simple life. He worked a steady job in the city, commuted daily from his modest apartment, and spent weekends catching up on errands. His dreams of success and achievement seemed distant, almost unattainable. That was until one evening while browsing an online bookstore, he stumbled upon a newly released title, "The Secrets to Swift Achievement: Unlock The Keys to Succeed Faster."

Curiosity piqued, Alfred bought the book and began reading it that very night. The first chapter spoke about the importance of setting clear, concise goals. Inspired, Alfred took a notebook and wrote down his ambitions, from career advancement to personal growth. The act of writing them down made his goals feel tangible, within reach.

The following chapters revealed practical strategies: the power of focused effort, the significance of time management, and the art of leveraging one's network. Alfred learned to prioritise tasks, eliminate distractions, and utilise every minute effectively. He started waking up earlier, dedicating the first hour of his day to self-improvement and strategic planning.

Alfred also learned about the value of mentors and collaboration. He began attending industry seminars, where he met seasoned professionals who provided invaluable insights. Their guidance helped him navigate challenges and avoid common pitfalls.

As months passed, Alfred noticed remarkable changes. His productivity soared, and his performance at work caught the attention of his superiors. Opportunities that once seemed elusive now came knocking at his door. His colleagues sought his advice, impressed by his newfound efficiency and success.

The final chapters of the book emphasised the importance of resilience and a positive mindset. Alfred faced setbacks, but armed with the knowledge from the book, he viewed them as learning experiences rather than failures. He remained steadfast, adapting his strategies and continuously improving.

One year after discovering the book, Alfred's life had transformed. He had achieved a promotion, expanded his professional network, and even started mentoring others. The secrets to swift achievement were no longer secrets but principles ingrained in his daily routine.

Standing in front of his window, looking out at the bustling city below, Alfred felt a deep sense of fulfilment. He had unlocked the keys to succeed faster, not by some magical shortcut, but through dedication, strategic planning, and the wisdom from a book that had changed his life.

We're quickly approaching next year and the end of another year. It is a time when many of us will set new goals for the next year. In the big scheme of life, the word 'many' means very few. I know, what a paradox! Many people consider making changes, but few truly follow through. I know you're reading this because you're one of the few who want to change their lives in some way and want to know the critical steps to success.

This is your time.

Keep your eye on the prize, but it is also vital to develop strong success habits if you want to break away from your old way of life, experience the success you deserve, and realise your goals. Some people agree that old habits are difficult to break. While this may be true, I encourage you to focus on what you can do to make this year a transformative year.

Too much, too soon.

Lack of planning and impatience result in disappointment. We strive to accomplish too much, too quickly, with insufficient information and preparation. This leads to mishaps, and when things don't go as planned and goals are missed, we become dejected and feel like giving up.

The key to unlocking the keys to success faster is one critical factor: continuous action. The deciding factor distinguishes those who thrive from those who stagnate. But let's be honest: maintaining consistency can be difficult. We struggle with procrastination and inconsistent motivation. Whether adhering to an exercise regimen, pursuing an educational objective, or completing a professional project, recognising the keys to constant action can help us reach our full potential and move forward.

This Book's Purpose

A manual designed to help you reach your maximum potential and achieve your goals efficiently and effectively. In this book, we will look at many tactics, approaches, and insights from psychology, productivity, personal development, and success studies.

In today's fast-paced environment, accomplishing one's objectives quickly is more important than ever. Whether you're looking for personal development, job advancement, or entrepreneurial success, mastering the art of quick accomplishment can make all the difference in reaching your goals.

Throughout the following chapters, we will look at the fundamental principles that support success, such as goal setting, mindset cultivation, productivity mastery, habit creation, resilience, connection building, and long-term success methods. Each chapter will include practical exercises, real-world case studies, and concrete approaches to help you implement these concepts in your own life.

In today's fast-paced world, where distractions abound and time is limited, the ability to focus and complete tasks quickly is nothing short of a superhero. Imagine using your mental energy like a laser beam, effortlessly propelling you toward your goals.
However, speedy achievement is more than just crossing the finish line swiftly; it is also about doing so with intention, integrity, and fulfilment. It's about matching your actions to your ideals, seeing challenges as chances for progress, and making meaningful relationships.

As you embark on this path to rapid success, I want you to approach each chapter with an open mind and a desire to engage thoroughly with the subject. Consider your personal goals, problems, and capabilities, then utilise the tools in this book to plan your road to success.

Regardless of your path, remember that you can change your destiny and live the life you want. So, let's dive in, learn the secrets to quick success, and unleash your full potential together.

Part 1

Setting the Foundation

"Success is not built on success. It's built on failure. It's built on frustration. Sometimes it's built on catastrophe."

Sumner Redstone

Any long-lasting construction is constructed upon a solid foundation. Just as a building needs a sturdy foundation to reach dizzying heights, any undertaking or initiative requires a secure footing to survive and persist. A solid foundation is especially important in our pursuit of long-term success. The value of creating good groundwork cannot be emphasised, whether in terms of personal development, commercial ventures, or relationships.

You're building your future. Or, at the very least, you're deciding how to strive toward the future you've always wanted actively! However, knowing where to start to lay the groundwork for your desired job might be difficult. You may not even be sure what you want to do yet! Earning a new degree or furthering your education might be the first step toward achieving your job goals. If you're new to online education or haven't been in school in a while, you may be anxious about returning to the groove.

A firm foundation serves as a safety net, allowing you to withstand the inevitable storms of any trip. Consider a business; one with a strong financial foundation is more likely to weather economic downturns. Similarly, an individual with a solid emotional and mental basis can better deal with life's obstacles.

A strong foundation frequently begins with a clear sense of purpose. When you understand your 'why,' your goals and decisions become more purposeful and consistent; consider the case of Steve Jobs, who started Apple to make technology available to everyone. This unshakable purpose created the foundation for Apple's success.

Success does not happen overnight. It's a path that takes discipline, good habits, and accountability. To succeed in any aspect of your life, you must first construct strong fundamental foundations. We'll look at the key components you need to develop to lay these foundations and set yourself up for success in life.

1. Determine your desired career by asking yourself some crucial questions.

When building something from scratch, you must have a clear vision of the result, as well as a plan on how to get there. When you build a house, you utilise blueprints to outline the "bones," or frame, of the structure. Do the same for your professional ambitions. Begin by establishing a list of what you want to accomplish, your key goals, and what you need to get done. If you're not sure where to start, ask yourself a few of the following questions:

- What do you enjoy doing? This could be a list in and of itself, but understanding what you enjoy doing will help you limit potential occupations that will bring you happiness.
- What specific activities do you enjoy that can lead to a job? You've made a list of things you enjoy, but can you make a profession out of them? Absolutely. Get specific and analyse what activities you enjoy and what occupations require you to engage in those activities.

Here's an example. You enjoy animals and taking care of them. You regularly volunteer at local shelters and aspire to work in animal care. You're also interested in business, and you enjoy leading and keeping things organised.

You've contemplated working in a veterinarian practice, but you don't want to watch the blood or the aftermath of surgery. You do not have to become a Veterinary Technician; the Veterinary Medicine industry also requires somebody to manage the business. Becoming a Vet Practice Manager may be the ideal profession for you!

- What skills do you need to attain the job you want? You are certain in the direction you want to pursue your career, but you are unsure whether you have the qualifications. Whether you wish to start a new career or advance in your existing one, there may be some talents you lack.

Look for job ads in your area that match your desired career or position. Browse the internal job boards to discover what qualifications similar occupations require. Skills and education requirements in several roles across different organisations will give you a good picture of what the industry is looking for generally.

- What education do you require? Return to the job postings you were scanning. Did they need candidates to hold a degree? A diploma? Certifications? While many jobs can start with hands-on experience and training, most employers require formal schooling or certification.
- Where do you see yourself in a few years? Perhaps you want to go to the corner office, or you simply desire a job that makes you

happy. Whatever your future vision is, you must first determine your ultimate aim. Knowing this allows you to set attainable goals. A plan can help you achieve your goals without wasting time looking for every opportunity.

Answering those questions can help you create a plan for accomplishing your goal. You may even begin the plan with one notion in mind only to discover that, after careful analysis, there is a better approach to get where you want to go.

Once you decide what to do, you must gather the necessary materials to begin construction. What tools do you keep in your toolbox for achieving success?

2. Create a durable future by utilising the appropriate resources.

Building oneself up is easier when you have the necessary resources and tools. When you need a screwdriver, you don't use a hammer, right? It is important to take your time and do it correctly if you want to start with a solid foundation you can rely on.

Steer clear of quick cuts that seem rewarding and efficient at first. Even while you can find yourself reaching your goals much more quickly, the actions you omitted along the road will eventually catch up with you.

This applies to all professions. After landing an entry-level job, you might be passed over for promotions and more responsibility if you miss a class or training your employer prioritises or the HR department mandates. Even though you do a fantastic job at your job, someone else took the time to master every step, which will make them seem more desirable to your employer when it comes time for a promotion. Remember the following inquiries:

What actions must you take to succeed in the career you desire? Speak with a familiar employee already working there. This could be a friend who currently holds the position you're aiming for, or it could be a mentor or supervisor at your current workplace.

How could they have arrived there? They are well-established in their field, so finding out how they got there will help you identify the steps you've already taken and the ones you still need to work on.

Remember to conduct your research. Ensure the skills and program you finish fulfil the requirements you identified in your job searches before enrolling in any course, certificate, or program. It's vital to ensure that your work to develop your abilities and resume will be relevant because different companies and institutions have different requirements.

If you're enthusiastic about achieving your primary objective, investing the necessary time now will help you prevent disappointment or failure later on.

3. Honour the little victories.

It's acceptable if success isn't always immediate. Small goals and milestones are crucial when developing your talents and résumé. They are the source of your motivation to pursue your primary objectives.

Make yourself weekly or even daily objectives. This might be anything from completing an exam each week to reading at least one portion of your study guide. Your little victory will boost your confidence and get you one step closer to achieving your objectives.

Make relevant goals for yourself to stay motivated and on course. A meaningful objective would encourage you to go closer to your destination and has some bearing, no matter how slight, on the tasks you must finish. One minor but significant victory in finishing your class, a step toward completing your degree, is completing a lesson in your study guide.

Remain responsible for yourself. Write down your objectives in a diary or planner. To ensure you meet each milestone, you can even use the goal tracker that can be printed out and downloaded. You'll find it easier to picture your progress if you write out your minor goals and explain how they fit into your overall plan.

4. Construct your future with assurance.

Whatever your ultimate objective, you must invest the time to create a solid and enduring foundation for success. Gaining confidence doesn't stop when you finish your degree or training course!

Your confidence in your abilities can be strengthened by talking to individuals in your sector, keeping up with pertinent information, listening to educational podcasts or audiobooks, and learning outside the classroom and via on-the-job experience. You can avoid being caught off guard in meetings or when speaking with your managers at work by feeling assured that you are informed.

You can be sure that your professional choice was the proper one for you, in addition to being sure you know what you're doing in your new position. Better yet, you can easily discuss your ambitions with a potential employer and bring a degree to support your claims about your expertise to the interview.

Penn Foster can assist you in beginning to acquire the fundamental abilities and confidence to accomplish what you love, whether you're just graduating from high school and searching for your ideal profession or trying to improve your existing circumstances in the industry. We offer anything from certificate programs to strengthen your CV to college degrees meant to get you ready for success in the real world.

We will examine various viewpoints on success and how it varies throughout individuals in Chapter 1 of this section.

Chapter 1

Defining Success

Success from Various Angles

Well, I think you've heard everything. Self-improvement books and publications, TED talks, inspirational speakers—you name it.
If the phrase "success" but, more significantly, "different" has any significance for you, continue reading.

In my professional setting of Africa, where I have done numerous trips, I have become weary from striving for what is commonly seen as a success. Like everyone else, I thought success came from a protracted selling process. You ultimately failed and did not sell. I'm afraid I, though, have to disagree.

You know, I get up at 6:30 every morning. Many of us will knock the alarm clock off under the bad, then knock it again to the trash can, and then back to the bad, but I managed to wake up! The daily workout was completed (I may have even finished first occasionally), and most importantly, I have once again demonstrated that I will never give up—not this morning, not ever.

I am using this thinking style: "What you set out to achieve, and the accomplishment of achieving it" is what success is all about. I apply it in business meetings, business development, and intercultural relationships. All of it consists of this. That being said, what makes my "Different Perspective of that word - Success" so unique? I, however, split up my little victories. Have you heard of "divide and conquer"?

Let's say we build reachable success by setting short targets! Now, let's revisit my "Selling" example. Divide it, please.

Suppose I were able to generate a lead! That is, reaching out to someone who I could sell via and who could end up being a devoted partner (also known as an agent). Subsequently, I effectively oversaw an account, adhered to a planned pipeline, traveled, met, and reached an agreement to divide actual future profit shares—in short, and I performed admirably. I was very successful so many times. It isn't easy to succeed in business growth, marketing, and sales, as you may already be aware.

As you can see, I succeeded one step at a time. I was getting closer to the result, which is selling, with each step.
We occasionally forget that we should pay attention to all of the "bus stops along the way" since we are constantly focused on the end results. Every move you take is a victory!

Saying, "I want to be the owner of 1 million dollars," would be a frustrating procedure if one didn't realize that he would have to go through other digits along the road, obtaining less stunning quantities eventually. Perhaps a never-ending process. If that aim were divided, it would lead to more attainable goals, more motivation from actual success, and—above all—greater enjoyment and self-belief throughout the journey.
I can see why some of us might think, "Well, that's not too hard. By employing this strategy, you're being cowardly." What's the matter, you know? Well done, everyone.
Let me give it a shot. In life, whatever you do, always divide and conquer. It might be anything from work to sports to attempting to start a

relationship with someone you want to go out with. Simply break down your missions and goals into manageable chunks. Recall that by adopting this mentality, you raise your odds of success while ensuring your failure because achievement is defined as "what you set to achieve, and the accomplishment of achieving it," one step at a time.

These days, it seems impossible to avoid the word success. Maybe partly because so many of us chase it with such abandon, because the internet says we should, we feel compelled to. While some people blog about it, some sit about it and hope it finds them, and others become obsessed with it.

Have any of us, though, taken a moment to consider what the word means to us? Not Google's or Webster's definition, but our own.
You can never know when you've arrived without a destination, no matter how significant your journey is. Said, if you're not sure what you want in the first place, you'll never obtain it.

I see a lot of people following a route in which they have little genuine interest. Once more, they didn't stop considering whether they wanted anything society says they should pursue and do in life.

Instead, they went out to chase and accomplish these goals. To find out later that they didn't and are now legally, emotionally, or professionally obligated to have them.

For me, achievement is defined as being able to read, write, and run when I get up every day. Success is having the freedom to pursue those interests whenever I want to, not just when I have the time or can fit them in around a ton of other "have" to-do tasks.

Success for me is knowing that I am happy with who I am and my work. It's not arriving home after a miserable day at work to find my house filled with hate, toys strewn everywhere, and an overflowing dishwasher.

It's unrelated to the amount of money in my pocket or the figures on my bank statement. Success does not equate to cash; money is merely one of its byproducts.

You can achieve success without ever having produced a dime, and you can accumulate wealth without ever accomplishing your goals. Since achieving your goals defines success, it is a personal experience.

However, I'll be the first to acknowledge that while having Fuck Though, it's not how prosperity looks in real life, having that kind of money would be fantastic. Personal happiness, or anything close to it, is what I consider to be the main component of success. While money can purchase many things for you, true happiness is not one of them.

To be successful means that my parents must be pleased with the person they perceive in me. It involves being a trustworthy individual who fulfills their commitments and someone my friends know they can count on. Good nutrition and a restful night's sleep are essential for success. They know that with my resources that day, I did my best.

Success, above all, is never allowing someone to tell me what success means or looks like. It involves making my own decisions and pursuing them with steadfast conviction. To me, having a purpose that defines who I am now is what defines success. Prior to having that stuff and continuing to be fundamentally dissatisfied, I believed that success was all about material possessions. That is ego and consumerism, not success. It all ends up seeming as ridiculous as it makes you feel to have thought any of it would eventually make you feel successful when you're alone in a room with everything.

So, surround yourself with success and experience what it's like! Feels fantastic!

The Definition of Personal Success is Crucial

This is the part of the book where we discuss personal success and its importance to us. Although everyone's definition of personal success is different, it is a strong motivator that pushes us toward realizing our potential and reaching our objectives. This section will look at individual success from various angles and explain why it's so important to us.

- A person's ability to achieve their goals and objectives—whether they have to do with their work, relationships, health, or personal development—can be considered their level of individual success. It includes the sense of fulfillment and achievement from conquering obstacles and achieving goals. While obtaining financial stability may be important to some, pursuing their hobbies and having a beneficial impact on society may be more important to others when it comes to personal achievement.

- Since it gives our lives direction and purpose, understanding and pursuing personal achievement is essential. It encourages us to aim for constant progress and assists us in setting meaningful goals. We can find ourselves aimlessly roaming without a sense of accomplishment or fulfillment if we don't have a clear idea of what personal success means to us.

- Enhancing our general pleasure and well-being also heavily depends on personal success. Our sense of confidence and self-worth is increased when we make progress and attain goals that are meaningful to us. Consequently, this enhances our mental and emotional health, resulting in increased life satisfaction and pleasure.

- Moreover, achieving success in one's life can motivate and inspire others. When we succeed and conquer challenges, we set an example for everyone around us. Our accomplishments can encourage others to follow their goals and have faith in their skills, resulting in a positive cascade of individual development and prosperity across the community.

- It is imperative to acknowledge that the notion of personal success is not universally applicable. An individual's definition of personal success may vary significantly from another's. It is a very subjective and intimate experience that ought to be characterized by each person's values, goals, and interests. It can be detrimental and cause feelings of inadequacy to compare our paths to personal accomplishment with those of others. Unlocking personal achievement requires embracing our individuality and concentrating on our development.

To demonstrate the importance of individual achievement, let's examine Alfred's story. A young businessman named Alfred decided to launch his own company. For him, achieving personal success meant starting a business that shared his beliefs and improved society. After years of tenacity and hard work, Alfred's company enhanced many people's lives and made a profit. His sense of accomplishment from reaching his objectives and having an influence stoked his enthusiasm and inspired him to keep developing.

In our lives, personal accomplishment is crucial because it gives us meaning, fulfillment, and direction. It is a very personal journey that is unique to each person and whose pursuit enhances our general happiness and well-being. Through comprehending and accepting our distinct journey towards individual achievement, we can actualize our complete capabilities and motivate others in the process.

Achievement is a big word. It has a plethora of diverse meanings. It impacts us whether we balance our personal health, creative endeavors, parenting, careers, or education. Achieving success can truly motivate us to complete tasks and meet goals in our lives. Why, therefore, is it crucial to establish your definition of success before pursuing your goals in many spheres of your life?

People define success for us. From a young age, success is the goal. Whether it's successfully uttering our first words or learning to walk. Surviving is the key to success. Every one of us lives in a culture that values success. It is a fact of life. You are unable to avoid it. That's even more motivation to consider what success means to you personally. My concept of success has changed significantly since I was in my early 20s and early 30s, and I am aware of this now that I am forty years old.

Don't let the culture of comparison distort your definition of success. I discuss comparison culture with friends and coach clients regularly. Comparing oneself to people around us, whether in person or virtually, comes naturally to us. Thus, wherever feasible, remember that you can't always evaluate yourself based on what other people are accomplishing or what makes them successful. It all comes down to the fact that each person has a unique story, which I will discuss later.

Success can also come from the little things. It's simple to think that success entails great things. Many people aspire to achieve great things, perhaps more observable or tangible. That's okay, but make sure your idea of success aligns with your values and way of life. Don't discount the less significant or unexpected victories. They might turn out to be the most significant ones. And speaking of values, well.

It all comes down to your values. When you're concentrating on achieving your goals, your values become extremely important. What matters most to you?

Success isn't just about possessions, it's also about emotions. When all material possessions are taken away, what remains in life that truly brings you happiness? Is it merely happiness, or is it your health? Is it a desire to assist others? Does it matter if you smile every day or have fun? List the top five values that you find most significant.

Not everything matters where you end up. Depending on the subject, the journey might be as important as the destination. When we set our sights too high, we lose sight of the experiences and accomplishments we have already achieved. We neglect to consider how things felt.

Which is more important, happiness or success? A lot of people believe that joy follows achievement. It should be the other way around, in my opinion, since pleasure makes you feel more successful. Success can be a fleeting emotion. That may be appropriate for you, but if it's what makes you happy most of the time, don't depend on it.

Your tale, your life...It would help to accept that your life and story will never be the same. This implies that your path to achievement and your trip will be distinct. The other week, I received a reminder to "stay in your lane" from a respected business founder. She emphasized the need to stay true to my strategy and plan and resist the want to get into other people's spaces and worry about their actions. I've come to realize that our little family's narrative and its puzzle pieces define our own and our kids' definitions of success. Our experiences—both good and bad—will enable us to understand what true success looks like..

Does winning necessarily equate to success? I have enjoyed being recognized for my efforts throughout my career. My upbringing was in a culture that values achievement highly. Perhaps this is why I like to work with people rather than against them. Over time, I've understood that growth is equally significant to success.

Goal-Setting by Beliefs and Ambitions

You can be more certain that you're working toward personally significant goals if your goals are in line with your values and desires.

You'll likely feel dissatisfied and detached if your objectives don't match your values and desires.

Understand the significance of matching your objectives with your values and the essential elements of collaborative leadership.

Getting our goals in line with our beliefs and ambitions is one of the most important things we can do to find purpose and direction in life. Living a life that aligns with your basic values and beliefs is your purpose, not just reaching goals and finishing tasks on your to-do list.

The motivation that propels us toward our purpose is ambition, and we are more likely to discover that aspiration and find joy in our endeavors when our objectives are consistent with our beliefs. To help you connect your objectives with your beliefs and create a more fulfilling and meaningful path, we will go over the essential steps in this part.

- **Contemplate your principles:** Taking stock of your priorities and values is the first step towards matching your aspirations with your values. Which values serve as your life's compass? What do you cherish most about your work, relationships, and personal development? You can recognize objectives consistent with your core beliefs by developing a deeper grasp of your values. An ambition to publish a book, for instance, can align with your beliefs if you respect creativity and self-expression.

- **Establish your goals:** The motivation that keeps us going and inspired to work for our objectives is aspiration. Examine your hobbies and interests, and focus on what makes you happy and fulfilled. The path becomes more fun, and the likelihood of success increases when your goals align with your dreams. Your feeling of purpose may be sparked if you aim to serve others by establishing a goal to volunteer frequently or launch a nonprofit.

- **Make significant objectives:** Setting meaningful goals for yourself is necessary after fully grasping your values and ambitions. Refrain from basing your aspirations on what others or society think you should accomplish. Rather, concentrate on what genuinely aligns with your goals and ideals. Setting objectives that are meaningfully in line with your personal beliefs might be achieved, for instance, by reducing your carbon footprint or launching a community recycling program if you value environmental sustainability.

- **Act consistently:** It takes regular activity and dedication to match your aims with your values; it doesn't happen overnight. Make a plan to achieve your goals by breaking them down into smaller, more doable actions. As you take action, stay committed to your goals and values, and periodically evaluate your progress to make sure you are still doing what is most important to you. Enjoying the trip is just as important as getting to your destination.

- **Accept adaptability and progress:** You must embrace flexibility and remain receptive to learning when you set out to match your objectives with your values. Our values can change throughout time or for us develop new interests along the way. Give yourself permission to change and refocus your goals as necessary. Recall that living a life that is true to your values and objectives is more important than strictly adhering to a set plan.

Aligning your goals with your values will help you find aspirations in your purpose. You may design a life that aligns with your principles by considering your beliefs, recognizing your dreams, establishing significant objectives, acting consistently, and embracing change. You'll feel inspired and fulfilled to follow your mission with zeal and excitement when your goals align with your values.

A fundamental element of collaborative leadership involves formulating a common vision that synchronizes the objectives and principles of all parties involved. A shared vision is an exciting and compelling picture of the future that unites people and inspires them to commit to, rather than just a declaration or catchphrase.

A common goal gives the partners in the project direction, inspiration, and a sense of purpose. It also acts as a manual for making decisions, fixing issues, and resolving disputes. In order to develop a shared vision, the following actions must be taken in a collaborative manner:

1. Determine the common ground:

The first stage is to ascertain the needs, interests, aspirations, values, and beliefs of the collaborators. Surveys, interviews, focus groups, brainstorming sessions, and other techniques that promote discussion and input can be used to do this. Finding common themes, patterns, and insights that arise from the various viewpoints of the collaborators is the aim.

2. Articulate the vision:

The next stage is to take the areas of agreement and turn them into a succinct statement that encapsulates the agreed vision. In addition to being upbeat, practical, and attainable, the statement should be challenging and motivating. It ought to address the queries, "What do we want to achieve?" and represent the values and objectives of the partners. What motivates us to accomplish it? How are we going to do that? The statement should be written in an approachable, clear style that is easy for everyone to read and comprehend.

3. Visualize the vision:

The third phase involves bringing the shared vision to life in a way that will captivate the participants' imaginations and feelings. A sketch, collage, logo, symbol, metaphor, narrative, or any other kind of expression that embodies the spirit and meaning of the vision can be used as the picture. The participants should utilize the image as a reminder and inspiration for their acts, and it should be widely shared and displayed.

4. Align the vision:

Aligning the vision with the partners' plans, strategies, activities, and behaviors is the fourth step. This entails making certain that the vision directs and informs the decisions and actions of the organizations or groups concerned and that it is congruent and compatible with their current mission, vision, and values. It also entails coordinating the partners' resources, positions, duties, and expectations and giving them the encouragement, criticism, and acknowledgement they require in order to realize the goal.

5. Review and change the vision:
The last phase is to periodically review and revise the vision, modifying it to fit the demands of the partners and changing circumstances. This entails keeping an eye on the development and results of the partnership, assessing its performance, acknowledging its achievements, and drawing lessons from its mistakes. It also entails asking for and taking into account the collaborators' opinions and suggestions, as well as revising and enhancing the vision as necessary.

Recall that you're more likely to feel content and happy when your goals are in line with your beliefs and passions. It also adds enjoyment and satisfaction to the process of reaching your objectives.

Now, moving on to Chapter 2 we will discuss the psychology of achievement, exploring in detail the mindset and belief systems, self-efficacy and confidence, and overcoming limiting beliefs. What are you waiting for? Let's get started!!!

Chapter 2

The Psychology of Achievement

The pursuit of achievement is a fundamental aspect of human nature. From personal goals to professional aspirations, understanding the psychology behind achievement is crucial for unleashing our full potential. This chapter explores key psychological factors that contribute to achievement, highlighting the importance of mindset and belief systems, self-efficacy and confidence, and overcoming limiting beliefs.

Mindset and Belief Systems

In this section, the terms belief system and mindset are used interchangeably. However, they are two quite distinct animals.

Mindset

A person's beliefs determine their thinking, which in turn affects how they interpret the world and themselves. It influences your feelings, ideas, and behavior in each given situation. It suggests that how you view yourself has an impact on your success or failure.

People can have more than one kind of attitude, according to some academics. A person's total attitude is composed of various types of mindsets, such as growth mindset, fixed mindset, abundance mindset, wealth mindset, poverty mindset, and positive mindset.

More generally, researchers have discovered that a person's attitude has a variety of functional consequences in several spheres of their existence. This involves acting as a filter, frame of reference, system of meaning-making, and pattern of perception, all of which can affect an individual's ability to perceive. A person's mindset is defined as influencing their potential for growth and is linked to three types of learning: transformative, vertical, and gradual, or horizontal. It is also thought that a person's mindset affects their conduct, as it is linked to both technical and adaptive leadership philosophies and phases of deliberate or implemental action.

A mindset may encourage the adoption (or acceptance) of prior choices, actions, or resources; this phenomenon is also referred to as groupthink or cognitive inertia. In situations when a dominant attitude is restricting or unsuitable, it could be challenging to break free from its hold on analysis and judgment.

A mindset is an internal representation of your goals, aspirations, and the subsequent course of action that will lead to success.

Your belief system is reflected in your current circumstances in life.

You have the mindset of a millionaire but the belief system of a poor guy, for instance, if you have been acting like a millionaire for a while but haven't been able to make any money.

Belief System

Everybody acts according to a set of beliefs. To succeed, it helps to know the main ideas that influence your work. For instance, you might decide against a job in active management if you think that equities markets are generally efficient.

You might decide against investing altogether if you think that money is the source of all evil!

Beliefs are difficult because they are imperceptible. Many of us become confused when questioned about our "beliefs operating system," just like the fish that is asked about his opinion of the water. We can't see it since it runs continuously in the background, much like Windows on a PC. But, our computer could become severely slow or even shut down if a virus infects the operating system. Similar to viruses that affect an individual's operating system and reduce their effectiveness at work, humans can also have bad thoughts.

Good thoughts, such as "I'm a talented and capable person," are supportive of our efforts at work and ought to be fostered. You won't be effectively served by negative views such as "Only suckers put in extra time at work."

Since we have thousands of beliefs, it is impossible for us to examine and assess them all. A lot of them are unimportant. (Although I don't personally believe in the Loch Ness Monster, it hasn't really affected my career.) Finding and giving priority to the ones that actually affect your work is crucial. Deal with the unhealthy ones and swap them out for more positive ones.

Alternately, deal with the ineffective ones and swap them out for productive ones. For instance, "We can win by hiring smart, hardworking people," is a common belief among active investors. Research indicates that better results call for more than this. (After all, how many businesses employ illiterate, slothful people?

What is a Belief System?

Beliefs alone do not constitute a belief system. The fact that the beliefs are tied to one another is what sets it apart. It's a set of values.
The network's constituent beliefs logically support one another and generally do not contradict one another, making it highly coherent but not entirely consistent.
Because of this, the system as a whole is likely to be impacted by the adoption of a new belief or the modification of an existing one, which may lead to a rise in the level of illogicalness.

Let us assume that the conviction that things change is a strongly held fundamental belief. Stated differently, it is inextricably linked to other beliefs whose validity depends upon it. Since many other beliefs must also change in order to restore the coherence of the system, the change in this instance is probably going to be quite disruptive.

There's a conflict between your belief system and mindset. Your belief system always prevails when your mindset and belief system clash.

Self-improvement methods and strategies assist you in aligning your belief system and attitude so that you can succeed in life. The peculiarity of self-improvement methods and systems is that, due to individual differences in belief systems, what works for one person may or may not work for another.

Try something new and different if using a self-improvement approach isn't assisting you in changing your beliefs the way you want them to.

The Impact of Beliefs on Mindset

Every choice is predicated on a belief. That is, we make decisions based on what we perceive to be true, or what we know to be true. Nonetheless, there are instances when we hold false beliefs. When logic and facts don't suffice, our actions are influenced by our beliefs, both intellectual and emotional.

How do our beliefs come about? Our belief systems are formed and shaped by the connections, experiences, events, and circumstances of our early years. But if we don't look at our beliefs and make them conscious, we can keep making decisions based on information that isn't true or accurate.

What steps can you take then to challenge your belief system?

- Take out your holy cows. It's not necessary for you to stick with a belief you've held your entire life. According to Stanford psychologist Lee Ross, people routinely overlook the contextual factors that influence behavior. This is referred to by him as the "Fundamental Attribution Error." Our tendency to blame our actions on "the way I am" rather than "the situation I'm in" is where we make the mistake.

Making up new scenarios is therefore the first step. Make a steep downhill slope and give yourself a shove instead of setting yourself up for daily struggle. Reduce the amount of friction on the trail and place numerous markers along it to indicate your progress.

- Form fresh routines. I worked as a coach with an executive in the construction sector last year who was experiencing anxiety due to difficulty setting priorities. He was simply not finishing tasks. In order to assist Peter see the moments when he was putting himself in a setting that exacerbated his anxiety, I asked him to take me through a normal day.

Peter claimed that when he checked his emails first thing in the morning, anxiousness set in. Peter was overwhelmed right away, which made it difficult for him to set priorities and ultimately led to him losing control of his day.

I didn't let Peter get away with saying, "That's just the way I am." Rather, I requested that he modify his circumstances and dissect his past achievements. He acknowledged that he had made additional folders for less important emails, which he would deal with on specific days and at specific times. To put it another way, he took charge and altered his circumstances, which altered his habits.

Get off behavior autopilot and stop doing what you're doing if it's not working.

Peter also took another action. He lessened the cognitive shock.

- Lessen the cognitive shock. Individuals dislike acting one way and thinking another. Therefore, it gets harder for people to not like the way they're acting after they take a modest step and start acting differently. In a similar vein, people start thinking of themselves differently as soon as they start doing differently, and when their identity changes, it supports their new behavior.

I assisted Derrick, the president of a tiny manufacturing branch of a much bigger company, in lessening his cognitive dissonance a few years ago. Through our engagement, I came to understand that Derrick was facing the possibility of losing three key members of his leadership team due to their inability to collaborate with Osman. Each related tales of Osman inciting strife, storming out of meetings, and generally mistreating his teammates. Osman was challenging for me to work with, and in the one and only instance in my more than 35 years of doing this work, he stormed out of a one-on-one meeting with me.

Derrick told me, "I know, Jennice, but the guy makes me so damn much money," when I brought up Osman's actions. I'm unable to fire him. Osman had lied on his application, a teammate who had worked with him at a prior employer revealed later in the day. Contrary to what he had stated, he was not a Ph.D. I told Derrick that he would either have to fire Osman or corporate HR would probably terminate him when I approached him with this knowledge.

Derrick's view that he was keeping the finest rainmaker on staff was justified, despite the fact that it went against the company's core values of honesty, decency, transparency, shared risk, and simplicity.

After firing Osman, Derrick saw a slight decline in revenue before being elevated to the position of corporate vice president. That day, Derrick caused some disruptions, but he also improved things. Derrick discovered that our ideas impact the way we think, which in turn affects how we act.

Whenever our words and deeds are less at odds, it gets easier to make tough decisions. We cannot behave otherwise than in line with our core values—the places where our beliefs and deeds align—when the stakes are great.

Our worldview and mentality are shaped by these unconscious beliefs, which also produce biases. We perform the necessary actions that increase our confidence and enable us to feel comfortable taking a chance when we proactively analyze our attitudes, prejudices, beliefs, and values.

But we tend to notice the negative rather than the positive because of our negativity instinct. Here, three things are happening: the tendency to misremember the past, calling it back to the "good old days" when in reality it was not; the belief that it is callous to suggest things are improving while they are still awful; and the constant barrage of terrible news. (When was the last time that an airline flight without a crash was reported? However, when a plane does crash, the news coverage of it lasts for several weeks or even months.)

People who mistakenly think that nothing is getting better may come to the conclusion that everything they have tried thus far has failed and lose faith in the things that do, in fact, work. All too frequently, customers come to me with a laundry list of things they tried and failed to achieve, forgetting to include all the things that made a small but meaningful difference.

Self-Efficacy and Confidence

One of the most important things you can do to bring about change in your life is to set goals.
But as most of us are aware, it may be very challenging to even decide to take the initial step and commit.

For what reason is that the case? Consider the following questions for yourself:

- Are you unable to take the initial steps toward reaching your intended goals for a specific reason?

- Is all you're doing is putting off doing what you know has to be done by putting it off?
- Are you concerned that there might be something there that you are blind to? Are any components missing?
- Are you concerned that maybe your goals and route are not the proper ones?
- Are you worried about your discipline and drive to follow through?

Yes, it is accurate; the reason motivation and self-control are on the list is that they are lacking rather frequently. But there's another component that you often don't realize is lacking. High self-efficacy is the missing component. One of the most frequent challenges I encounter while dealing with clients is low self-efficacy.

What is Self-Efficacy?

A person's confidence in their capacity to finish a task or reach a goal is known as self-efficacy. It includes a person's self-assurance in their ability to manage their conduct, have an impact on their surroundings, and maintain motivation while working toward their objective. Self-efficacy can exist in a variety of contexts and domains, including relationships, the workplace, education, and other crucial areas.

Do you believe you can overcome a difficulty and achieve your objective, or do you give up in defeat? Do you have faith in your own ability to overcome obstacles in life, or are you more like the tiny train engine from the beloved children's book "I think I can, I think I can!" You most likely have a high level of self-efficacy if you have a tendency to persevere in the face of difficulties.

Self-efficacy is crucial since it affects both how you see yourself and your ability to accomplish your life's objectives. Albert Bandura's social cognitive theory, which emphasizes the importance of social experience, reciprocal determinism, and observational learning in the formation of personality, is centered on the idea of self-efficacy.

As to Bandura, self-efficacy is a component of the self-system, which is made up of an individual's abilities, attitudes, and cognitive capabilities. This system has a significant impact on our perception of and reactions to various circumstances. A crucial component of this self-system is self-efficacy.

Basics of Self-Efficacy

"The conviction in one's capacity to plan and carry out the actions necessary to handle potential circumstances" is how Albert Bandura characterizes self-efficacy. A person who believes they can achieve in a certain situation is said to possess self-efficacy. These kinds of ideas influence people's thoughts, feelings, and behaviors.

One of the most researched subjects in psychology is self-efficacy since Bandura's groundbreaking 1977 paper, "Self-Efficacy: Toward a Unifying Theory of Behavioral Change," was released. Why is self-efficacy a subject that psychologists and educators are discussing so much these days?

Self-efficacy has been shown by Bandura and other researchers to have an impact on motivation, behavior, and psychological states. What objectives we seek, how we achieve them, and how we evaluate our own performance are all influenced by our level of self-efficacy.

Our perception of our own potential for success influences our thoughts, behaviors, and feelings regarding our position in the world.

The Part Self-Efficacy Plays

Almost everyone can name things they would like to change, things they would like to do, and goals they would like to reach. But most individuals also understand that it's not exactly so easy to carry out these plans. According to research by Bandura and colleagues, a person's self-efficacy significantly influences how they approach tasks, goals, and obstacles.

Being highly self-sufficient is beneficial. Individuals that have high self-efficacy:

- Becoming increasingly engaged in the activities they engage in
- Increase their level of dedication to their hobbies and pursuits.
- Recover swiftly from disappointments and failures.

- Consider difficult issues as chores that must be completed.

On the other hand, low self-efficacy can have various negative consequences. Individuals that have low self-efficacy:

- Steer clear of difficult assignments
- Feel that challenging assignments and circumstances are beyond their reach
- Concentrate on your shortcomings and unfavorable results.
- Lose faith in one's talents quickly

Comparison of Self-efficacy, Self-esteem, and Self-confidence

Although self-efficacy and self-esteem are commonly conflated, there are significant differences between the two. What distinguishes self-efficacy from self-esteem? Self-esteem is your regard for your value and worth, whereas self-efficacy is your belief in your ability to achieve in various circumstances.

Are self-efficacy and self-confidence synonymous? Despite their similarities, there are a few key differences between the two names. A person's general belief in themselves in all situations is called self-confidence, which is more generic. Contrarily, self-efficacy is more situational and context-specific. One can have poor self-efficacy in some areas (like athletics) and great self-efficacy in others (like academics).

Studies indicate that self-efficacy is a predictor of self-esteem. Stated differently, an individual with strong self-efficacy also typically has high self-esteem, and vice versa.

In What Ways Does Self-Efficacy Grow?

Dealing with various events, tasks, and circumstances during early infancy helps us develop our feelings of self-efficacy. But self-efficacy doesn't stop growing in childhood; rather, it keeps changing as people grow older and gain new knowledge, experiences, and abilities.

Four categories of self-efficacy

The four processes that lead to the development of self-efficacy are psychological reactions, social modeling, mastery experiences, and social influence.

Psychological Reactions

Our emotional and personal reactions to events can significantly impact our self-efficacy. Various factors, including stress levels, bodily reactions, emotional states, and moods, can influence a person's perception of their talents in a given circumstance. A person who has great anxiety before giving a speech in public may grow to have low confidence in their ability to speak in public.

Still, Bandura emphasizes that" how emotional and fleshly responses are perceived and interpreted matters more than their raw intensity."

People can feel more capable of handling tough or challenging activities if they learn to reduce stress and boost their mood.

Social Modeling

Another significant element of self-efficacy is observing others accomplish a job. Bandura states that," Seeing people analogous to oneself succeed by sustained trouble raises spectators' beliefs that they too retain the capabilities to master similar conditioning to succeed."

Mastery Experiences

"Having mastery experiences is the most efficient approach to build an intense feeling of effectiveness, according to Bandura. When we do a task successfully, our self-efficacy increases. Nonetheless, a goal or challenge that is not sufficiently met can erode and impair self-efficacy.

Social Influence

Additionally, Bandura claimed that people could be convinced they possess the abilities and skills necessary for success. Think back to a time when you were able to accomplish a goal because of a supportive and encouraging comment from someone. Receiving verbal support from others enables people to overcome self-doubt and concentrate on giving the task at hand their all.

High Self-Efficacy Example

What, then, is the precise manifestation of strong self-efficacy? You may undoubtedly recall a few instances from your own life, such as when you felt extremely powerful. Individuals can feel competent in various contexts, including work, school, friendships, parenting, sports, and hobbies, or they can feel competent in a particular domain.

Here are a few instances of high self-efficacy:

- A person having difficulty managing a chronic condition believes that, with hard work and adherence to their doctor's advice, they can get back on track and improve their health.
- A pupil who has faith in their ability to study the material and perform well on an exam.
- Someone who just accepted a job offer in a role they have never held believes they can pick up the skills necessary to do the job well.

When it comes to health psychology and how individuals handle their diet, health, and sickness, self-efficacy might be crucial. For instance, people trying to stop smoking may find it easier to stick to their goals if they have a high feeling of self-efficacy.

A person's levels of self-efficacy can affect a variety of behaviors, such as adhering to an exercise regimen, managing chronic pain, maintaining a weight reduction plan, quitting alcohol, and following an eating plan.

Studies have also demonstrated the beneficial effects of high self-efficacy teachers have on academic outcomes, such as student motivation and achievement.

According to Bandura, there are several ways in which self-efficacy can enhance one's sense of well-being. For example, even in adversity, they maintain their optimism and self-assurance.

People who possess strong self-efficacy perceive challenges as opportunities rather than obstacles, which leads to a greater innate interest in the activities they undertake. Failure and difficulty don't equal defeat for these people; instead, they spur them on to more effort and innovative problem-solving techniques.

Low Self-Efficacy Problems

Individuals with poor self-efficacy frequently perceive challenging jobs as dangers they should avoid. They also frequently avoid making objectives and show little dedication to the ones they create.

When they face obstacles, they often give up easily. They are more prone to feel depressed and like failures because they lack confidence in their abilities to succeed. Stressful circumstances can also be very difficult to handle, and those with poor self-efficacy tend to be less resilient and unlikely to recover.

Self-efficacy is the antithesis of learned helplessness. It can happen when someone feels helpless to influence the course of events. Rather than seeking ways to influence the result, they give up and act in a submissive manner.

Analyzing the Strength of Self-Efficacy
Take a moment to answer the following questions informally to gauge your level of self-efficacy:

- Do you believe that if you put in the necessary effort, you can handle challenges?
- Do you think you can accomplish your objectives?
- Do you think you could handle unforeseen circumstances?
- Are you able to recover from stressful situations quickly?
- Do you think you are capable of solving problems when they arise?
- Do you persist in your efforts when things appear challenging?
- Are you adept at maintaining composure amid the chaos?
- Do you function well under duress?
- Do you often feel accomplished rather than overwhelmed by the work still to do?
- Do you think that perseverance will finally be rewarded?

You likely have a high sense of self-efficacy if you can say "yes" to most or all of these questions.

Increasing Self-Efficacy

Fortunately, you can develop and enhance self-efficacy as a psychological talent. Begin by considering how you may apply Bandura's sources of self-efficacy to your situation. Self-efficacy can be attained in several ways, such as by practicing positive self-talk, seeing your mentors in action, accepting positive comments, and recognizing your accomplishments.

Honor Your Achievement

Experiences with mastery are essential for the development of self-efficacy. Bandura found that this was the only strategy to build a strong sense of self-belief.

One can develop a strong self-belief when they achieve success in anything. Conversely, failure might weaken these emotions, especially if you still develop a sense of personal efficacy.

But the best kinds of success aren't always the ones that come easily. If you have a lot of easy success, you could discover that when defeat eventually comes, you give up easier. Thus, make an effort to create objectives that are challenging but attainable. Even though they will require effort and persistence, if you do them, your confidence in your skills will grow.

Examine Others

Vicarious experiences gained from peer modeling are another crucial way to build and maintain self-efficacy, according to Bandura. Seeing others work hard and achieve might boost your confidence in your capacity for success.

How much the model resembles you is one issue that greatly influences how effective this method is. Your sense of self-efficacy will likely rise in response to your observations if you feel more alike than different.

Look for Convincing Verdicts

Getting encouraging comments from other people might also boost your feeling of self-efficacy. In the same vein, refrain from seeking input from those you know are more inclined to be critical or negative about your work.

It can be motivating, for instance, if your doctor tells you you are following your diet plan well. Getting input from mentors, friends, medical professionals, and other respected individuals can boost your self-confidence.

Negative remarks can frequently have a potent undermining effect, but positive social feedback can be beneficial for bolstering your sense of efficacy. Although Bandura argued that social feedback is not sufficient on its own to increase self-belief, it can be a helpful tool when you need a little extra support.

Be Aware of Your Thoughts and Feelings

Before a difficult event, if you become anxious or stressed out, you may not feel as confident in your ability to complete the work at hand.

Seeking strategies to control your thoughts and feelings about the goals you have set for yourself is another method to increase your sense of self-efficacy.

<u>Overcoming Limiting Beliefs</u>

Have you ever told yourself that you should avoid doing anything because you're not good at it? These ideas frequently stem from pessimism and anxiety, which prevents us from taking advantage of fresh chances.

You're not alone if you've thought anything like this. Many professionals and even business owners battle with self-limiting attitudes that can prevent them from reaching their full potential. To overcome limiting beliefs, the secret is to understand how to recognize them.

Limiting beliefs has an impact on teamwork in a variety of ways, including culture, performance as a whole, and team productivity. Nine of the most prevalent self-limiting ideas have been compiled, along with strategies for dispelling them in day-to-day living.

A classic metaphor describes a baby elephant being chained to a fence post. The newborn elephant pulls and pulls, but it cannot break the rope or the fence. It eventually gives up and accepts its fate. The little elephant is stranded.

However, the elephant soon matures into a large, adult animal with enormous legs, a massive tusk, and a swirling trunk, and it can easily escape the fence if it so chooses. However, the adult elephant stays chained to the fence because it mistakenly thinks it is an immovable object and that it will never be able to escape.

Limiting beliefs: what are they?

A mindset or belief about oneself that confines you is called a limiting belief. These beliefs are frequently untrue charges that you level at yourself, and they can have many detrimental effects.

False beliefs, known as limiting beliefs, keep us from achieving our objectives and fulfilling our dreams. Limiting beliefs might prevent you from pursuing significant goals, such as putting in an application for your ideal job or locating and ending a relationship. Additionally, they can prevent you from engaging in pointless activities like skydiving while wearing only your panties or sampling that strange Scotchberry ice cream flavor that resembles baby puke in a cone.

What we consider to be reasonable behavior is constrained by our beliefs. My moral conviction prevents me from robbing the next automobile that passes, à la Grand Theft Auto. This restrictive belief is most likely a useful one to hold. Thus, it is possible to argue that not all limiting ideas are harmful. To be more precise, we require certain limiting ideas to prevent us from doing foolishly.

However, some restrictive ideas needlessly prevent us from becoming the people we want to be. These restrictive beliefs keep us where we are without realizing it, much like the elephant that stays glued to the fence post. In this article, I'll be talking about these limiting ideas.

For instance, you'll probably turn down any chance to impart your expertise to others in a group environment if your limiting attitude is that you're not very good at inspiring speaking. Alternatively, you might believe that speaking in front of an audience increases your chances of failing. This results from your limited potential due to preconceived beliefs about your speaking abilities.

Limiting beliefs can also trap you in the wrong frame of mind, making it difficult for you to take advantage of new possibilities and experiences in life and severely harming your mental well-being. This is why it's critical to address unconscious prejudices and improve self-awareness and self-esteem. Having preconceived notions about other people makes it difficult to deal with them successfully, which eventually lowers the caliber of your output.

How restricting ideas affect a team's performance

Opposing ideas can lower team morale and creativity in the workplace regarding restricting beliefs. Let's say you are developing a new procedure, but you lack the confidence to suggest a more effective fix for the issue. Undoubtedly, the result won't be novel.

As a team leader, you may unleash your team members' creativity and participation by assisting them in addressing their limiting beliefs. Retaining these unfavorable notions can impede people from thinking creatively and beyond the box to generate fresh, original ideas. Nothing hinders team success more than repurposing previous concepts.

Real growth occurs at these daring times. Thus, each team member must have enough self-confidence to push past limitations. To enable your staff to perform and be at their utmost best, it is crucial to promote positive thinking in the workplace.

Nine (9) typical instances of limiting beliefs

Any self-deprecating views that prevent you from developing personally are considered limiting beliefs. Knowing the most prevalent limiting beliefs will help you recognize them when they occur, whether through verbal views, body language, or defense mechanisms.

To help you with your professional self-improvement, here are (9) typical instances of limiting beliefs that you should identify and address right away:

1. " I am immature enough to be a director," rather than" I am too old."
2. " I do not have enough time to invest in myself," is my statement.
3. " I am not smart enough to lead this meeting," you say.
4. " I don't have enough experience for such a major career move," could be the response.
5. I will no way be successful" I will no way be successful in my profession."
6. "I don't have adequate rich people to take pleasure in my life," I said.

7. You tell yourself," I will in no way be among the most effective on the platoon."
8. " I am not talented enough to get a creation," one might say.
9. I will in no way make a great leader" My lack of confidence prevents me from ever being a great leader."

These kinds of beliefs are universal and stem from a place of fear. The intention is to enable you to recognize and challenge limiting ideas to break free from your comfort zone.

To keep yourself safe, you might be tempted to convince yourself that you're not good enough or that you never will be, but ultimately, these ideas limit you from achieving your goals and pushing your team to be the greatest.

The secret is to be able to identify your own limiting ideas when they surface and then utilize that awareness to change the way you view yourself. Encouraging your team to follow suit will help you improve as a manager.

What leads to Limiting beliefs?

Although there are many causes of limiting beliefs, they all originate from your brain's need to keep you safe from potential suffering. Past experiences, fear, and impostor syndrome are a few examples of these triggers.

Limiting beliefs frequently originate at an early age and gradually change and reshape as you go through life and encounter new things. Limiting beliefs can keep positive new beliefs from forming, whether because of a traumatic incident that made you fear similar encounters or because you're afraid of what lies ahead.

Understanding the reasoning behind your limiting beliefs and taking steps to manage them can be achieved by understanding their source. There are a variety of other strategies you can use to get over your concerns at work.

How to overcome limiting beliefs in the workplace

Self-limiting beliefs can be corrected when you recognise them, but it takes time and effort to understand how to overcome them. A few pointers can be helpful when examining how to get over these anxieties at work and how to teach your team to do the same. It is up to you how you employ the four approaches, but each one can assist you in overcoming limiting beliefs in the workplace.

1. List your beliefs and make a note of them.

Recognizing your limiting ideas is the first step towards changing them. Rather than being something you express aloud, these beliefs frequently appear as thoughts in your mind. Putting these ideas down on paper will make it easier for you to distinguish between fact and fiction and will reveal how false they genuinely are.

Jotting down your ideas in a journal will assist in reducing any tension related to the notion. You might also ask yourself if this idea is pertinent to the task you have to do in the next ten minutes. If not, shut your journal and record your pessimistic ideas there.

Although this exercise is performed alone, you might motivate your group to practice it daily. If team members feel comfortable sharing limiting beliefs with colleagues, you can also set up a weekly meeting where they can do so. Team members have an opportunity to build trust as a result. To set an example, make sure the experience is entirely voluntary, but also plan to participate yourself.

2. Evaluate the precision

If jotting down your ideas isn't sufficient, it can be beneficial to assess whether or not your opinions are based on truth or fiction.

You may see your limiting beliefs for what they indeed are by delving into their core. The next time a false belief pops into your head, stop, consider, and evaluate it. Consider whether it is self-limiting and whether any complex data support your belief. Consider whether the thought results from a previous experience or a dread of the unknown.

Your productivity might suffer greatly when you strive for perfection, and when things aren't going as planned, it can make you want to give up. One strategy to counter this is to ask your teammates for comments. Ask yourself if you are unsure if your limiting notion is true. This helps you disentangle the facts from the narratives you tell yourself since you're getting an unbiased viewpoint that isn't influenced by your own.

3. Make use of uplifting words

Positive affirmations are one of the most effective strategies for dispelling limiting thoughts. Repeating affirmations to oneself helps you believe in yourself more.

To transform self-limiting ideas into positive self-beliefs, employ positive affirmations. Reframe negative beliefs about yourself, such as "I'm not good enough for a promotion," by convincing yourself that you are a dedicated worker who deserves success. Making any negative thoughts positive can help you combat them. Saying things aloud to yourself or others might help reinforce the belief. However, there are many other ways to do this.

This is a technique that you can use to stop self-limiting ideas before they start, or you can incorporate it into your routine to utilize when negative sentiments arise. Reframing self-defeating thoughts can take many forms.

- Modifying the statement" I can not handle this design" to the words" I have the capabilities essential to succeed in whatever I do."
- Modifying" I warrant the sufficient time to devote to myself" to" I can change my schedule and concentrate on the most vital effects to me."

You may train your mind to perceive the advantages instead of the negatives in everyday situations by changing how you frame issues.

4. Keep going

Finally, if limiting beliefs start to seep in, never give up. Recall that you are not alone. Even highly regarded leaders and entrepreneurs have restricted views.

It's crucial to push past the limiting notion and keep progressing despite it. One of the most essential traits of a leader is never giving up on yourself or other people.

Even though it can be simple to feel depressed during a negative thinking cycle, ignore restricting ideas by taking some time for yourself. Sometimes, all you need to start moving more optimistically is a breath of fresh air.

5. Have faith in both your group and yourself.

Everyone experiences self-limiting ideas, so know that you're not alone if you do. It's crucial to learn how to get over limiting beliefs and concentrate on the good rather than getting rid of them. You may alter your life by changing your perspective.

To foster good self-perception in the workplace, your team must be assured and encouraged to realize their full potential. Your team can connect on tasks and strengthen one another using team communication tools.

Part 2

Goal Setting and Planning

"Goal setting is the compass that guides our journey, and planning is the map that ensures we reach our destination with purpose and precision. Together, they ignite the fire within us to turn dreams into realities and aspirations into achievements."

Jason M. Traver

Chapter 3

Setting Smart Goals

Every facet of life and business has goals because they give direction, drive, emphasis, and clarity on what matters. You give yourself something to aim for when you make goals. Setting goals is aided by using SMART goals. "specific, measurable, achievable, realistic, and timely" are abbreviated as "SMART." To help you focus your efforts and improve your chances of reaching your goal, a SMART objective includes all of these elements.

Specificity, Measurability, Achievability, Relevance, Time-bound

Lack of a goal can cause you to go up and down the field your entire life without scoring.— William Copeland

Have you ever felt that, despite your best efforts, nothing is happening? Looking back over the last five or ten years, you might not see much improvement in your abilities or accomplishments. Or maybe you find it challenging to envision how you'll be able to achieve your goals over the following several years.

Many people spend their lives bouncing between jobs or working long hours in an attempt to accomplish more, but in reality, they rarely get anything done. By establishing SMART objectives, you can improve your chances of reaching your life's goals by streamlining your thoughts, concentrating your efforts, and efficiently using your time and resources.

We'll define SMART goals in this part and examine how you can utilize them to accomplish your goals.

- **The Method of Specificity**

Clarity and direction can only be given by establishing clear objectives. Instead of aiming for a general goal like "increase sales," try something specific like "increase monthly sales by 20% within six months." You can better gauge your progress along the way and establish a framework for your actions by outlining your goals in detail.

You won't be able to focus your efforts or feel entirely driven to reach your objective if it isn't clear and distinct. Plan your aim by attempting to address the following five "W" questions:

1. What am I hoping to achieve?
2. Why is achieving this aim crucial?
3. Who takes part?
4. What location is it?
5. Which limitations or resources are at play here?

➢ As an illustration

Let's say you are a marketing executive who wants to advance to the position of head of marketing. A particular objective would be, "I want to gain the skills and experience necessary to become head of marketing within my organization so that I can build my career and lead a successful team."

- **The Method of Measurability**

Determining the success of your endeavors requires measuring your progress. Setting up measurable metrics enables you to monitor your progress and make corrections. If your objective is to close ten deals a month, for example, it will be simple to track your progress and pinpoint areas that need work. Measurable objectives drive you to push yourself harder and recognize your accomplishments.

Setting quantifiable objectives will help you monitor your progress and maintain motivation. Evaluating your progress enables you to remain committed, fulfill commitments, and experience the thrill of approaching your objective.

A quantifiable objective should answer queries like:

1. How much?
2. In what number?
3. How can I tell when it's finished?

➢ As an illustration

If your goal is to become head of marketing, you may gauge how close you are to achieving it by estimating how long it will take to finish the required courses and accumulate the necessary experience in five years.

- **The Method of Achievability**

Setting lofty objectives is vital, but it's also critical to ensure they are doable. To establish reasonable expectations, evaluate your abilities, the resources at your disposal, and the state of the market. Just enough stretching should make you feel challenged but not overpowered. You can stay motivated and prevent yourself from giving up on your dreams by creating realistic goals.

For your objective to be successful, it must also be achievable and reasonable. Stated differently, it ought to challenge your capabilities while maintaining feasibility. Setting attainable goals can help you find resources or opportunities you may have missed, but that can still help you reach them.

Typically, a feasible goal will provide an answer to queries like:

1. How can I achieve this goal?
2. In light of other limitations like monetary considerations, how feasible is the objective?

➢ As an illustration

With your current experience and credentials, you may need to consider if it is practical to acquire the abilities necessary to become head of marketing.

Do you have enough time, for instance, to finish the required training? Do you have access to the resources that you need? Are you able to afford it?

Avoid establishing objectives that are under the control of another person. "Get that promotion!" for instance, is contingent upon the actions of the recruiter and the other applicants. However, it is entirely up to you to "get the experience and training I need to be considered for that promotion."

- **The Method of Relevance**

Relevance is the degree to which your objectives and long-term vision coincide. Every objective you choose should support your overarching professional goals. If your goal is to become the best luxury Realtor in your community, for instance, concentrate on establishing objectives that will enable you to specialize in high-end properties, cultivate relationships with wealthy clients, or advance your understanding of trends in the luxury market. This alignment guarantees that each step will bring you closer to your ultimate goals.

Making sure your objective is essential to you and that it fits in with other pertinent goals is the aim of this phase. While everyone needs help and support to reach their goals, it's crucial to maintain control over them. Thus, ensure that while your plans help everyone go forward, you are ultimately in charge of accomplishing your objective.

The answers to these questions can be "yes" for a relevant goal:

1. Does this seem like a good idea?
2. Is now the appropriate time?
3. Does this align with our other needs or efforts?
4. Am I the best candidate to accomplish this goal?
5. Does it make sense in the socioeconomic context of today?

➢ As an illustration

Even though you may aspire to become your company's head of marketing, is it the correct time to pursue the necessary education or certifications? Are you sure you are the best candidate for the position of head of marketing? Have you thought about your partner's objectives? Would it be more challenging to start a family, for instance, if you completed training in your spare time?

- **The Time-bound Approach**

Being time-bound is essential for keeping accountability and attention. Objectives without a deadline lose their effectiveness since they can be left unfinished. Setting deadlines makes it easier to stay on course and assess your development. Creating a sense of urgency and increasing the likelihood that long-term goals will be completed within the intended timeframe are two benefits of breaking them down into smaller milestones.

Every goal needs a target date to give you something to work toward and a deadline to concentrate on. This SMART goal criterion component prevents daily responsibilities from superseding your long-term objectives.

A time-bound goal typically addresses the following queries:

1. When?
2. In six months, what can I do?
3. In six weeks, what can I do?

4. What actions may I take today?
➢ As an illustration

As we previously discussed, obtaining the necessary training or experience may be required to develop the skills to become head of marketing. How much time will it take you to learn these abilities? Do you need more training to meet the requirements for a particular exam or qualification? Setting realistic deadlines to meet the lesser objectives required to reach your ultimate goal is crucial.

In the Real Estate industry, defining and achieving goals is crucial to success. Using the SMART goal framework—which stands for specific, measurable, achievable, relevant, and time-bound—will boost your output and produce outcomes. Recall that time-bound deadlines provide urgency, specificity brings clarity, measurement records progress, achievability sustains motivation, and relevance links goals with your vision.

To revolutionize your real estate career and lead yourself to unmatched success, set SMART goals. Accept the power of goal-setting and see how your aspirations come to pass. As always, we are here to assist you in reaching your objectives!

Creating Goals That Work

Writing successful goals is essential to achieving success and personal development. On the other hand, how we phrase our objectives can significantly impact how likely we are to succeed. Well-written goals offer direction, clarity, and a plan of action.

Setting goals on paper is similar to drawing a map to your destination. You know exactly where you want to go, what you want to accomplish, and the necessary measures. Furthermore, it gives you a feeling of motivation, accountability, and focus. However, that is merely the very beginning. You might be surprised to learn how exhilarating it is to put your aspirations in writing.

Consider that setting writing goals is like making a vision board for yourself. You can use art and creativity to express yourself. To make it entertaining and exciting, use various colors, pens, stickers, and drawings. It's also a fantastic chance to let your imagination run wild and embrace your inner child. You don't have to limit your dreams to what you believe is achievable.

Writing out your objectives also allows you to look back on your journey, which is an enjoyable exercise. You get to see your progress, accomplishments, and areas for improvement. It's an excellent approach to recognize your achievements and learn from your mistakes. Furthermore, it's a fantastic justification to give yourself a small treat each time you reach a goal.

Not to mention the scientific advantages of putting your goals on paper. It has been demonstrated to raise the possibility of reaching them; did you know that? In a Dominican University study, participants who listed their goals on paper had a 42% higher chance of succeeding than those who didn't. The researcher was Dr. Gail Matthews. That is a noteworthy distinction! Writing out your objectives forces you to use a different part of your brain than simply thinking about them. You generate a drive and sense of commitment that encourages you to act.

In this instance, we will examine the craft of crafting achievable goals and advance us toward achievement by examining essential tactics.

- **Be Particular and In-Detail**

Being explicit and detailed while establishing goals is one of the most important things to remember. Ambiguous goals are devoid of the focus and precision required for successful execution. You can establish a definite target to strive for by outlining your goals and providing the necessary data.

- **Make Use of Positive Words**

Our motivation and mindset are significantly influenced by the language we choose in our goal statements. Use language that is constructive and emphasizes your goals rather than your avoidances. Positive reinforcement of beliefs, proactive attitude, and motivation are all enhanced by positivity.

- **Give Them a Measure**

Measurable objectives offer a concrete way to monitor development and assess achievement. Establish clear goals or benchmarks that will help you monitor your progress and maintain motivation. Tracking development gives one a sense of accomplishment and motivates one to work harder.

- **Establish Due Dates**

Deadlines give goals a sense of urgency and make them easy to put off. Setting reasonable deadlines for your objectives helps you prioritize your work and instills a sense of urgency and accountability. Set deadlines to ensure consistent action toward your goals by giving you focus and organization.

- **Divide Them Into Doable Steps.**

Significant objectives may be demoralizing and cause inertia. Divide things into more manageable and less intimidating smaller, doable tasks. With this strategy, you can move closer to your final goal while making small steps forward.

- **Write in the first person, present tense.**

Use the present tense to express your aims as though they are happening. By using visualization and affirmation, this strategy helps you believe you can achieve your goals and strengthens your belief in your abilities. You can establish a strong sense of commitment and synchronize your subconscious mind with your desires by reaffirming your goals in the present tense.

- **Continual Evaluation and Illustration**

Setting down your goals in writing is a continuous practice rather than a one-time event. To keep your written goals top of mind and to bolster your motivation, look over them regularly. Imagine yourself accomplishing those objectives and the feelings and benefits that follow. You can stay motivated, stay focused, and take action by using visualization.

- Accept Adaptability

Because life is dynamic, things could change while you're traveling. When defining your goals, embrace flexibility and make required revisions. Stay committed to your overall aspirations while adjusting to your aims in response to new circumstances or insights, and being adaptable guarantees that your objectives stay pertinent and in line with your changing course.

- Seek Support and Accountability

Having a mentor, accountability partner, or close friend know your goals will increase your chances of achievement. They can hold you responsible for your behavior and offer support and direction. Maintaining direction and conquering challenges can be significantly aided by the outside viewpoint and support.

In summary

Setting and completing objectives is a skill that helps us realize our potential. We establish a strong foundation for success by being explicit, using positive language, quantifying them, assigning deadlines, breaking them down, writing in the present tense, routinely reviewing and visualizing, embracing flexibility, and demanding accountability.

By developing our ability to write goals well, we can reach our full potential, build drive and focus, and open the door to achieving and experiencing life-changing experiences. Now, grab a pen, apply these techniques, and set off to achieve your goals.

Dividing Objective Into Doable Stages

Dividing your objectives into manageable phases is one of the most crucial parts of implementing your business strategy. This will assist you in maintaining accountability for your progress, motivation, and focus. It will also enable you to evaluate your progress and modify your action plan as necessary.

But, it might be challenging to break down your objectives, mainly if they are long-term, complex, or ambitious. How do you decide what to focus on first, where to begin, and how to keep track of your progress? This part will cover various strategies and tactics to assist you in turning your objectives into doable actions that will get you closer to your intended result.

You might use the following procedures to translate your objectives into doable steps:

1. **Establish SMART objectives.**

SMART stands for Specific, Measurable, Achievable, Relevant, and Time-bound. These are the standards that will assist you in establishing precise, attainable goals that complement your vision and mission. Instead of saying, "I want to grow my business," you might say something like, "I want to boost my monthly income by 10% in the following six months by establishing a new line of goods and increasing my advertising networks."

2. Divide your objectives into more manageable sub-goals.

Your SMART goals can then be divided into more achievable, smaller sub-goals that will act as checkpoints along the way. You can split your overall goal into smaller objectives, such as "research and develop a new product line," "create a marketing plan for the new product line," "launch the new product line and promote it to existing and potential customers," and "monitor and evaluate the sales and feedback of the new product line," if your objective is, for instance, to increase your monthly revenue by 10% in the next six months.

3. Give each sub-goal a task and a due date.

You can give particular tasks and deadlines to each sub-goal that will assist you in achieving your primary goals once you have divided them into smaller ones. Assign tasks like "conduct a market analysis to identify the needs and preferences of your target audience," "brainstorm and test different product ideas and features," "finalise the product design and specifications," and "prepare the product prototype and packaging," for instance, if your sub-goal is to research and develop a new product line. To stay motivated and on target, you can also give yourself deadlines for each activity.

4. **Make a schedule and a plan for your assignments.**

Once you have your assignments and due dates, you may make a strategy and timetable for them that will enable you to manage your time and resources efficiently. To assist you with this, you can utilise tools like planners, calendars, to-do lists, and project management software. A weekly or monthly plan that lists the actions you must do for each sub-goal, the time and resources you must allot to each work, and the expected results and deliverables for each activity is one example of a plan you may make.

5. **Monitor and evaluate your development and outcomes.**

Finally, to make sure that you are making progress toward your goals and are headed on the right path, you must periodically monitor and assess your outcomes. To assist you with this, you can use tools like dashboards, reports, and feedback forms. You can monitor and evaluate your sales and revenue information, such as customer satisfaction and retention rates, product performance and quality, market share, and competitive edge.

In addition, you can treat yourself to a celebration of your accomplishments and hard work. Should you face obstacles or failures, you might examine the underlying reasons and implement remedial measures to surmount them. You can also modify your plan, tasks, sub-goals, and goals to take advantage of new possibilities or adjust to changing conditions.

Chapter 4

Creating Action Plans

Will your dream become a reality? And how can you stay as clear of obstacles and issues as possible on this journey? A well-thought-out strategy of action.

A meticulously planned strategy that specifies the exact tasks, assignments, and resources required to accomplish a goal is called an action plan. It is pretty helpful for project management in general.

Making an action plan is similar to planning a cross-country route. It is the tactical blueprint that delineates each action, choice, and detour required to get to your final destination.

You're not just shooting in the dark when you have a well-thought-out action plan; instead, you're moving toward your objectives with deliberate, informed steps.

An action plan is a tactical instrument that delineates the precise actions, assignments, and objectives required to accomplish a specific goal.

Its main objective is to give individuals, groups, or organizations a clear path and guidance to successfully and economically achieve their objectives.

Action plans simplify monitoring progress and keep on course by breaking down complicated tasks into manageable, actionable components.

Furthermore, action plans are essential for encouraging team members to be accountable and coordinate their efforts. By establishing roles and due dates for every project or milestone, they ensure that everyone is aware of their obligations and the overall timetable, minimizing confusion and fostering better teamwork.

Action plans also aid in budgeting, risk management, and resource allocation by allowing stakeholders to anticipate problems and make backup plans.

An action plan's overall goal is to turn vague objectives into specific actions that may be taken to increase their likelihood of success and measurement while guaranteeing that the resources and initiatives are made in the direction of the desired outcomes.

Setting Task Priorities

The culture in which we live exalts busyness. But what are you occupied with? Setting priorities for chores can be challenging when everything appears essential. But to be effective and prevent burnout, you must have the ability to concentrate on what matters most.

Task Prioritization: What Is It?

Prioritizing tasks involves ranking them according to their significance and urgency. The objective is to increase your productivity and time management skills by arranging and concentrating on what needs to be done.

Setting priorities frequently entails putting off a work you wish to accomplish in favor of handling a more challenging or demanding one. Setting priorities for your tasks is a process that may be aided by several methods, strategies, and pointers that can help you concentrate better and better manage your time.

Typical Procedures for Task Prioritization

work prioritization can be achieved by identifying the various factors involved in a given work. Once you know which tasks are most important, you may put them in order of importance and decide when and how to complete them.

Create a list of all the tasks that are still pending. Make a list of any assignments or chores that occur to you to see how much work lies ahead of you.

Recognize Deadlines: Include the list of task deadlines. By doing this, you can more successfully divide your urgent work from less urgent chores.

Estimate the Time and Effort: You can more accurately determine a task's priority and design a strategy for completing your list if you know the resources required to finish each work.

Establish which tasks are the highest priority. This ranking should be based on the tasks' projected completion times and deadlines. Knowing which jobs are most important and urgent can help you prioritize them and choose what has to be done first.

Finish Highest-Priority Tasks First: Occasionally, the task with the highest priority is also the hardest. You can manage your time and priorities more effectively if you finish the most important things before accomplishing what you would instead do.

Keep Yourself Adaptable: Your responsibilities' requirements could sometimes alter; for example, a deadline could get pushed back or reduced, or an assignment might be eliminated. Maintaining flexibility will help you prioritize your tasks and make the most progress on your to-do list.

Regularly review and assess your tasks: Maintain a record of your assignments and due dates. Maintaining your to-do list can help you finish activities that are urgent or vital, make sure you don't forget anything, and eliminate items that aren't as critical or urgent.

How to Set Task Priorities at Work

Know what needs to be done and when it needs to be done at work so that you may prioritize your tasks. If you'd instead work on other projects, you might find it challenging to complete high-priority assignments.

Establish Due Dates for All Tasks: Give each task a big or small deadline. You might need to ask your coworkers for advice if a task doesn't already have a set deadline.

> For instance, you might receive an email from a coworker asking you to check a presentation when possible. You might need to work with your colleague to consider the due date of the presentation as well as any other unfinished business on your list because there isn't a set deadline.

Give Yourself Five Minutes of Willpower: One of the biggest obstacles to remaining focused and effective is getting started. Starting a difficult task (or personally boring) might be intimidating and cause one to put it off. If you give yourself five minutes to concentrate on the activity, you'll probably discover that five minutes becomes more time, and you'll get more done and possibly finish the assignment.

> For instance, you may be afraid of a long assignment and the deadline is approaching. When you look at a blank page and say, "I'm just going to work on this for five more minutes," you'll probably discover that you've already made a

strategy for the task and are feeling prepared to finish more.

Concentrate on One Activity at a Time: Multitasking is ineffective and less productive than concentrating on a single activity. Even though multitasking could seem like an excellent way to spend your time, if you don't do well on numerous things, you might end up wasting time.

Envision yourself in a meeting where you can reply to unanswered emails. The meeting's conversation fades to background noise as you compose your emails. As a result, you need to be reminded to respond to a colleague's direct query. Following the meeting, you also discovered that one of your emails was sent to the incorrect recipient and had other mistakes you must correct before sending it again.

Connect with Your "Why": Whether it's the reason you have a specific job, the objectives you hope to accomplish, or your personal beliefs, understanding your "why" can help you prioritize your responsibilities. It will be simpler to decide which of your chores should come first on your to-do list the more you can relate to the items on your list and how they suit your objectives and sense of self.

> ➤ Consider the scenario where you recently started a new job and want to establish a reputation for dependability and diligence with your supervisor and coworkers. There are several things you need to finish, one of which you said you would finish for a colleague. You decide to complete this assignment first since it will satisfy your need to be regarded as a conscientious and reliable person.

Methods for Setting Task Priorities

There are numerous methods for setting priorities that can help you increase performance and productivity, such as making a to-do list and stopping outside distractions. You can effectively organize and finish your unfinished activities by using the following strategies.

- **Make a list of things to do.**

Make a to-do list that lists all of the things you still need to complete and gives you a summary of them. This will assist you in monitoring and visualizing the chores that are required of you.

Creating a daily to-do list might help you stay organized and fulfill deadlines.

> Example: Your mind is constantly racing with a seemingly endless list of things that need to be done. It doesn't seem easy to finish this list, and you'll have to rely on your memory to remember the many tasks and requests. Sort your ideas and write out each assignment. Making a list helps you see your progress and acknowledge that your chores have an end.

- **Matrix of Eisenhower Priorities**

You can use the Eisenhower Priority Matrix to prioritize your projects according to their importance and urgency. The matrix's four quadrants are intended to help viewers understand a task's priority level.

> Example: You feel overburdened with many things to complete today. Utilize the Eisenhower Priority Matrix for every assignment to determine which ones are the most critical and urgent. By doing this, you become aware of the duties that you should plan out and do yourself and those that you should delegate to others. It's possible that you can eliminate specific jobs as well.

- **ABCDE Approach**

Each work is given a letter value according to the ABCDE method: an A is the highest priority and must be completed first; an E is the lowest priority and can wait until later.

> Example: You wake up on Monday morning with a list of things that need to get done. Making a brief document is one of those chores you keep putting off in favor of other duties. However, there is not much time left, and you have been requested to call a meeting, which will require much planning. The brief document is due on Tuesday, and the conference is scheduled for this Friday. When applying the ABCDE approach, you give the brief paper a value of A and the meeting preparation a value of B because they can be addressed later.

- **Chunking**

By finding the commonalities among the items on your to-do list, the chunking technique makes the most of your time and productivity. Rather than multitasking, you can accomplish more work quickly and efficiently by grouping related tasks. This is a more organized and concentrated way to finish your to-do list.

➢ Example: You have a list of things you must finish at work, and your manager and coworkers keep asking you to do more. Use the chunking technique to record each task and request. Examine your list and note any commonalities between the functions (such as communicating with clients, messaging, calling, and scheduling meetings). By grouping these duties, you may accomplish them more quickly and efficiently since you will be more focused and in the client-communication mentality.

- **1-3-5 Approach**

You can tackle activities with clarity and attention by rethinking your daily to-do list using the 1-3-5 method. List the nine things you want to get done that day. There should be one enormous task, three medium-sized chores, and five little tasks out of these nine. Utilizing the 1-3-5 method to arrange your to-do list will help you better manage your time at work and complete your duties on time.

➢ Example: You've been feeling unorganized lately. You think you are focusing on too many more significant projects and ignoring the more minor, equally vital chores because of the imbalance in the activities you finish. Reorganize your workday by deciding to spend less time on more significant projects so that you can complete jobs of all sizes. This can be done by applying the 1-3-5 strategy. Make a plan for the day that entails finishing one major project, three medium-sized chores, and five minor jobs rather than devoting the entire day to more significant undertakings. You'll feel less stressed and be more productive with this strategy.

- **How to Get Things Done (GTD)**

The five pillars of David Allen's productivity consulting method, Getting Things Done (GTD), are capture, clarify, organize, reflect, and engage. By putting your tasks on a to-do list, you may capture your thoughts and manage them more effectively. Next, you deconstruct more complex activities and eliminate irrelevant ones to make your list of chores more manageable.

Next, arrange the tasks on your list by grouping and classifying them according to similarity and urgency. Regularly review and update your lists as you work to ensure the items remain accurate. Finally, take on the tasks head-on to finish them.

> Example: You take on a new role at work and are overwhelmed by the work ahead of you. You have to research every aspect of your new department, meet with multiple individuals to get advice, and complete onboarding responsibilities. Get things done on your to-do list by using the GTD method. Put every task on paper first, then divide the more difficult tasks into smaller, more doable ones. After that, group the tasks on your list according to commonalities. You'll need to regularly review your list to ensure your duties meet your needs because your role is dynamic and fast-paced. You can better concentrate on and finish your chores when you have a clear plan for your work.

- **Consume the frog.**

Eat the Frog is a metaphor for doing the most challenging and significant assignment before beginning any other activity. This is probably the chore you loathe and avoid doing the most. You can increase productivity by completing your most difficult and important task first.

> Example: You receive a reminder from a colleague to go over a draft at the start of the day. You would instead finish your tiny

jobs than read through the long draft. However, you choose to take on the review. Both you and your colleague feel glad when the review is finished, and you can move on to minor duties for the remainder of the day.

- **Recognize Your Diversions**

Distractions fall into two primary categories that can reduce productivity. The most accessible distractions to manage are those that originate from our surroundings; you may do this by taking small steps like clearing your desk of clutter or removing your phone from your workspace. Distractions from the environment that become more noticeable and operate as a harmful stress-reduction strategy are known as procrastination distractions. Procrastination can increase stress levels and hinder us from doing our work efficiently.

You can avoid procrastinating by first being aware of — and minimizing — the distractions in your surroundings.

> Example: Your phone buzzes as you're trying to conclude a report. With your cellphone positioned next to your

computer, every notification is visible. You find yourself checking a news notification while you're supposed to work on your report, and then you spend a lot of time on your phone. You can't focus on your report and feel sidetracked even after putting your phone down. Put your phone away and switch it off before you keep scrolling through posts. This eliminates distractions from your work so you can focus on it.

- **The Warren Buffett Two-List Approach**

Writing down 25 of the most significant objectives now in your thoughts is part of Warren Buffett's two-list method. Choose five of the 25 goals that you feel are most important for your life. These objectives could pertain to other aspects of your life, job, or both.

Create two lists with this list:

I. Most Important Goals: Emphasize the most vital objectives to your life.
II. Avoid At All Costs: Determine which objectives prevent you from achieving your long-term priorities.

➢ Example: You've always had many goals for your life, many of which will require years of dedication. You've considered a career in medicine, but your goals are to return to school to get your MBA, work as a business professor, and advance in your current position to become a marketing director. Along with many other personal objectives, you also want to start a family and be as involved as possible.

➢ You list 25 of your most important life objectives using Warren Buffett's two-list method. Once you've calculated your 25, you circle the five that most closely correspond with your overall goals. You go around earning an MBA, moving up to become a marketing director, starting a family, putting money down for a comfortable retirement, and working four days a week in order to have additional time to spend with your family.

➢ You choose to dedicate less time, if any time at all, to achieving the objectives on the Avoid at All Costs list by doing this. You'll have more time to work toward your top five goals.

- **The Ivy Lee Approach**

The Ivy Lee technique, created more than a century ago by productivity guru Ivy Lee, demands you to prioritize your day by adhering to a set of guidelines.

The following are the Ivy Lee method's rules:

I. Every workday, at the end of the day, list the six most critical things you still need to get done.
II. To make sure your to-do list for tomorrow starts with the most important things first, rank the six items according to significance.
III. Try to finish all of the tasks in order the following day.
IV. Remain concentrated on each work and refrain from switching to another before completing the current one.
V. Create a fresh list of six chores to finish the next day at the end of the workday. Don't forget to add a task to the list for the following day if you don't finish it.
VI. Carry out the procedure again.

➤ Example: The amount of responsibilities and assignments you have at work overwhelms you. You have a PowerPoint deck that has to be finished immediately, a client meeting that needs to be prepared for in a few days, you need to investigate and recruit people for an impending conference, and you also need to write many descriptions for new training materials. You must reassess your workload to ensure that you finish your top priority.

Using the Ivy Lee method, you list the six things you think are most important to finish tomorrow at work. The assignments are listed in order of preference. You rank finishing the slide deck as your top priority, followed by looking into participants as number two, contacting them as number three, and getting ready for your customer meeting as number four. You want to concentrate on writing two of the many descriptions you have to write for the final two spots.

You take each task one at a time at work the following day, careful not to switch between or multitask. You feel much more successful than the day before when you discover that you have completed five of the six jobs. You make a fresh list of six things to do the following day, remembering to include the assignment description you could not finish.

Proven Methods and Strategies for Setting Task Priorities

There are several strategies you can employ to assist you in prioritizing your chores. Make use of your time and cross things off your list by putting some of Phoebe Gavin's suggestions below into practice:

- **Encourage Emotional Awareness:** Sometimes, emotions might get in the way of finishing necessary tasks. To prevent procrastination-causing coping techniques, be aware of your feelings, both toward the work at hand and in general. You may focus on your duties, even the most challenging ones, by developing more robust and healthier coping strategies with the support of greater emotional awareness.
- **Break Down Big Jobs:** To make large jobs more reachable, break them into minor, more doable activities. This shows advancement on the more significant task at hand as well.

- **Minimize Environmental Distractions:** Distractions from the outside world can make a work seem impossible to finish. Steer clear of distractions like your phone, email, instant messaging windows, and anything else you could find yourself grabbing for rather than the task. Eliminating external distractions might enhance your ability to concentrate on jobs that are of utmost importance.

Here are some more helpful professional hints and tips:

- **Apply the Pareto Principle:** This theory states that 20% of your efforts should yield 80% of your results. You can more skillfully prioritize your work to meet your objectives and get the desired outcomes by keeping this idea in mind.

- **Use a Scheduling Tool:** By doing this, you can ensure you don't forget any crucial or urgent chores by keeping track of your assignments and due dates. You can prioritize your time and remain productive if your tasks are structured.

Assign chores: If the amount of work on your to-do lists keeps you from focusing on the most crucial aspects of your work, consider assigning tasks to a colleague. This will assist you in gaining more time to work on the duties most vital to your position.

Time-Management Techniques

Many of us have trouble managing our time or how we decide to utilize and arrange it. By prioritizing things that will have the most significant impact and working more quickly effective time management enables us to make the most of each day.

Effective time management techniques vary for various people. If you are a graduate student, you might decide to handle your time differently than a mother who works. A color-coded calendar could appeal more to a visually oriented person than a printed to-do list.

What are some methods for managing your time?

The practice of deliberately organizing and regulating the amount of time spent on particular tasks to maximize productivity is known as time management. You could be accustomed to creating lists of tasks to complete, assigning yourself tiny prizes for completing them and setting deadlines.

To achieve your goals, you must decide what you need to do, when you need to finish, and which chores to complete. This is the essence of time management.

You will know you have effectively managed your time if you prioritize high-value, goal-oriented chores, complete them ahead of schedule, and make time to live a healthy lifestyle. But how is that accomplished?

Yes, by employing effective time management strategies.

You may be more productive and efficient with your time, make better decisions faster, and complete more tasks in less time and effort by adhering to a set of guidelines and concepts known as time management strategies.

The capacity to motivate oneself is one of the most critical components of time management. It requires work to develop positive habits and find motivation, which will help you work and live more productively.

Understanding existing tactics and best practices will help you establish healthy routines and behaviors. You can test them out in your own life and determine which ones suit you best.

Many time management strategies exist that are based on acknowledged best practices for time management, including:

- Jotting down your to-do list for today
- Completing critical and pressing duties first
- Setting aside time for regular and essential chores as well as breaks
- Effective stress reduction
- Appropriate team leadership
- Monitoring the status of a project and spotting delays

The majority of time management strategies address one or more of the points mentioned above; you may choose your plan by considering the areas in your routine that you would like to see improved.

In addition, you should consider your individual time management style and the time management abilities you still need to work on. Additionally, you can select specific time management strategies for your job to help you better plan your workdays.

Time management advantages

An example of a balanced, healthful lifestyle that can result from effective time management is:

- lowering tension
- Boosting vitality
- Reaching objectives more quickly
- Setting priorities for what matters
- Getting more done in less time
- Cutting down on procrastination
- Increasing self-assurance
- Progressing in your profession or studies

The most effective time management strategies

Which method works the best for improving time management?

Whether you must schedule your work, study, or goal-tracking time will mostly rely on your needs.

We review the top ten time management strategies you can attempt in the area below.

1. POMODORO

You divide your work into 5-minute breaks and 25-minute work intervals, or Pomodoro. You take a 20-minute pause after four cycles.

The Pomodoro technique, created by Francesco Cirillo, was named for the Pomodoro-shaped kitchen timer he used to monitor his productivity.

Time Management Abilities Enhances:

- Good organizing
- Control of stress
- Staying away from distractions
- Condensing on a single matter at a time
- Establishing priorities
- Saying "No"

PROBLEMS IT SOLVES:

- Poor scheduling,
- Ignoring breaks
- Taking on multiple tasks at once
- Deadlines that were missed

HOW POMODORO FUNCTIONS:

- Set a 25-minute timer for yourself.
- Use these twenty-five minutes to concentrate on your assignment.
- As soon as the alert sounds, stop.
- Take a five-minute respite.
- Follow the break with another twenty-five minutes of work.
- Take a 20-minute break after four cycles of 25/5 minutes each.
- Continue doing this until the assignment or project is completed.

THE BENEFITS OF POMODORO

- More accurate time estimations for the task.
- Set a fixed work hour, and you'll be more productive.
- Taking regular pauses reduces burnout and enhances performance.
- Pomodoros are a simple tool for monitoring productivity and profitability.

THE DRAWBACKS OF POMODORO

- Once the allotted 25 minutes have passed, you must cease working. If you are performing exceptionally well, this will not help you.

- Observing set intervals: You might not benefit from the recommended 25-minute sessions.

2. KANBAN

A kind of time management that allows you to visually watch the progress of your projects by tracking the transfer of work between columns with different labels.

Taiichi Ono of Toyota Automotive used this method in the 1960s in Japan to help boost manufacturing effectiveness and production.

Time Management Abilities Enhances:

- Good organizing
- SMART goal formulation
- Appropriate assignment of tasks
- Centralizing on a single topic at a time
- Problems it resolves:
- Taking on multiple tasks at once
- Deadlines that were missed
- Poor scheduling

HOW KANBAN FUNCTIONS

- A whiteboard and sticky notes, a pen and paper, or project management software are your options.
- Establish the columns after deciding how many stages your activity or project will have. For instance, you can arrange jobs inside a project throughout various stages by creating four columns:
- Backlog: this is where you list all of your tasks and ideas. After that, you determine which chores should go into the To Do column and which may wait.
- You will work on the items listed under "To Do."
- These are the projects you are working on right now, marked as In Progress.
- Completed: duties you've completed.

KANBAN'S ADVANTAGES

- No one-size-fits-all template exists, so you can alter the tenets to suit your requirements.
- Simple visual depiction of your project progress that captures the entirety of your work environment.
- You can divide the project into smaller, more doable tasks and monitor each one's advancement throughout.

- The group will probably focus on completing their jobs faster so that the "Done" column can be reached.

KANBAN'S DISADVANTAGES

- There isn't a single template that works for everyone, so making a Kanban board can take time because you have to choose how many columns to include and what to call them.
- Regarding relevance and urgency, Kanban doesn't directly assist you in organizing your work.
- Given that there is no time component and that the only way to gauge progress is by moving between columns, it could be challenging to estimate when your team will complete the tasks (and project).

3. GETTING THINGS DONE

A five-step process that helps you generate ideas for your chores and turn them into a simple to-do list.

David Allen popularised the concept of Getting Things Done (GTD).

Time Management Abilities Enhances:

- Good organising
- Establishing priorities
- SMART goal formulation

PROBLEMS IT SOLVES:

- Poor scheduling

THE PROCESS OF GETTING THING DONE

- Please take note of every task that comes to mind and capture it.
- Make the assignment more straightforward by deciding if it can be completed in an achievable amount of time and if there are specific stages you can follow.
- Arrange: group assignments into categories and provide them background information (e.g., home, office, request from Tom).
- Consider your tasks occasionally and ask yourself, "What's the next step?" Is it that noteworthy to execute it this week?
- Engage: Begin working on your chores after you have noted them, determined which

ones are actionable, correctly filed, and evaluated them.

ADVANTAGES OF GETTING THINGS DONE

- You'll maintain perspective on your chores, responsibilities, and projects.
- Once you've got every assignment you can think of, you'll have a clear brain.
- GTD can help you increase productivity in both your personal and business life.

DISADVANTAGES OF GETTING THINGS DONE

- To move forward with your task, you must exercise your willpower because GTD doesn't offer any advice on handling distractions.
- Tasks are arranged according to context rather than project, which could confuse individuals accustomed to organizing functions according to their projects.
- A list with too many items may not be helpful because you won't be as likely to organize your day well.

4. **CONSUME THAT FROG.**

The goal of this time management strategy is to prioritize your tasks. You choose your most critical or least desirable task (your "frog") and work on it first thing the following day. You can go on to other duties for the day when you have completed your "frog," but not before.

You may have been putting off this activity because it's boring, demanding, or complex, but it needs all your focus because of its significance or difficulty.

Time Management Abilities Enhances:

- Good organising
- Establishing priorities
- SMART goal formulation

PROBLEMS IT SOLVES:

- Poor scheduling
- Taking on multiple tasks at once
- Deadlines that were missed

HOW THAT FROG GETS EATEN

It is necessary to classify jobs according to their priority and identify them accordingly:

- Task A: Must be completed first, or repercussions may occur.
- Task B: Is the second most crucial task that needs to be completed; it should come first. It's still essential but less significant.
- Work C: You could complete this work, but failing to do so would not have any adverse effects.
- Task D: Is something you should ideally assign to a third party and use this time for Task A.
- Task E: Is one you can skip because it's unnecessary.

ADVANTAGES OF EATING THAT FROG

- You'll be motivated and energized to complete the other tasks in your daily schedule if you start the day with the most important or least desirable task.
- Setting priorities for tasks gets easier.
- You can do more fun things with the remainder of your day.

DISADVANTAGES OF EATING THAT FOGG

- It was a challenging and disheartening start to the day.

- If your most essential task varies during the day, it could be stiff and unworkable.

5. USING A TIME BOX

Time windows, or timeboxes, are assigned to activities; you work within them and conclude them after the allocated time has elapsed. Timeboxing is utilized in project management since it frequently involves set deadlines.

While timeboxes are 25-minute sessions, timeboxing is a more flexible alternative to the Pomodoro technique because it doesn't have a set duration.

James Martin provided the method's first detailed explanation.

Time Management Abilities Enhances:

- Good organising
- Staying away from distractions
- Concentrating on just one speciality at a time
- Establishing priorities

PROBLEMS IT SOLVES:

- Missed deadlines
- Poor scheduling
- Taking on multiple tasks at once
- Ignoring breaks

THE OPERATION OF TIMEBOXING

- Put together an inventory of all of your duties and actions.
- Determine your objectives for these tasks and what you hope to achieve.
- Give a task more time if it's significant and demands intense concentration (e.g., one or two hours).
- To make a challenging activity simpler to handle, break it up into smaller, more manageable tasks and give each one a shorter time limit (such as 20 to 30 minutes).
- Working your way down, begin with your first task.
- Don't continue working on a task after the allotted time has passed.
- Have a rest.
- Take stock of your accomplishments.
- Look at the various time slots on your calendar.

ADVANTAGES OF TIMEBOXING

- It is Ideal for many little jobs; once they are organized into timeboxes, it will be simpler to manage them and stay on top of them.
- Since deadlines are crucial, your attention will be directed toward accomplishing as much as possible before the timebox closes.
- Because they will have to move on to the next activity on the timetable, natural perfectionists will have less time to fine-tune every aspect.
- Timeboxing allows you to concentrate on one task simultaneously because it prohibits multitasking.

DISADVANTAGES OF THE TIME BOX

- When you become engrossed in a task, it is detrimental to quit working on it when the allotted time runs out.
- It may be challenging to stick to a strict plan established by timeboxes when you account for unforeseen interruptions such as phone calls.
- You could not be using timeboxing correctly. Timeboxes that are too short could force you to quit before you've fully completed a task. When a timebox is too long, you risk losing focus or beginning to

put things off in an attempt to extend the timebox.

6. TIME BLOCKING

You set aside time on your calendar to work on a particular task or activity.

Elon Musk is credited with popularising this time management strategy.

Time Management Abilities Enhances:

- Good organising
- Staying away from distractions
- Concentrating on just one speciality at a time
- Establishing priorities
- SMART goal formulation

PROBLEMS IT SOLVES:

- Deadlines that were missed
- Poor scheduling
- Taking on multiple tasks at once
- Ignoring breaks

THE OPERATIONS OF TIME-BLOCKING

Time blocking has 4 stages:

1. The phase of planning
   01. Prioritise and define your tasks and activities.
2. The phase of blocking:
   01. Give each activity a certain amount of time, either minutes or hours, and record the days, start times, and end times of each task in your calendar.
   02. The time block can be longer—90 minutes, for example—or shorter—10 minutes, for example. This is contingent upon the task's level of priority.
   03. Give critical projects more time on your calendar and schedule them for when you're most productive.
   04. Set aside time during the day when you are least productive for less crucial chores.
   05. Note the day, the start time, and the end time on a calendar.
3. The stage of acting:
   01. Work on your priority task, which is usually the first task you do each day.
   02. Ascend via your timetable.

03. Incorporate scheduled pauses in between time chunks.
04. Keep an open mind while creating your time-blocking schedule. If given an urgent task, set aside enough time and go to work.
4. The stage of revision:
01. Make changes to the timetable for the other tasks you have scheduled for that day if a task takes longer or shorter than anticipated.

ADVANTAGES OF TIME BLOCKING:

- A thorough method of monitoring your workday.
- It works well with Cal Newport's concept of deep work since it requires you to set aside a specific time each day to focus on a particular task.
- You'll experience an improved sense of control over your workload.

DISADVANTAGES OF TIME BLOCKING

- Unexpected events could cause schedule disruptions.
- Similar to Timeboxing, you can miscalculate your time and wind up rushing

to beat the clock during a tiny time block or putting off tasks until a time block that is too long.
- Scheduling time slots in your calendar for your daily tasks takes time.

7. INBOX-ZERO

This is a method of email inbox management that aims to maintain an empty or almost empty inbox.

Merlin Mann is a productivity specialist who created the methodology.

Time Management Abilities Enhances:

- Staying away from distractions
- Concentrating on just one speciality at a time
- Establishing priorities
- Control of stress
- Good organising

PROBLEMS IT SOLVES:

- Poor scheduling
- Taking on multiple tasks at once

HOW TO USE INBOX-ZERO

To get to inbox 0, you must:

- Please choose a time of day and stick to it for working on inbox management.
- Turn off notifications, and close the email tab in your web browser.
- Set email priorities:
    01. Instantly reply to emails that are most relevant to you and that you can swiftly respond to.
    02. Emails that will take longer to respond to should be moved to a "needs a response" folder. You should set aside time in your "manage inbox" for these responses.
    03. Select the messages you can assign, then send them to the other team members.
    04. Eliminate and save unsolicited or outdated texts.

ADVANTAGES OF INBOX-ZERO

- It is an excellent technique for handling a heavy inbox.

- Reduces the number of unseen emails, which hinders you from locating your critical correspondence.
- Centered on reserving inbox management for a designated time to prevent email distractions during the workday.

DISADVANTAGES OF INBOX-ZERO

- It is time-consuming because there are a lot of emails to forward, archive, and delete.
- It solely addresses inbox management; hence, it must be used with other time management strategies, such as those that emphasize task and project management.
- This is problematic for those who communicate by email with clients and coworkers—critical emails could be misplaced.

8. WHO'S GOT THE MONKEY?

This approach is primarily intended for project managers but can also be applied by others who strongly focus on work delegation. You have to think about how to handle chores like monkeys.

Three (3) varieties of "monkeys" and time management exist:

1. Boss-imposed time: tasks that the superior demanded.
2. System-imposed time: inquiries and requests from coworkers.
3. Self-imposed time consists of the things you choose to do. It can be used for your projects and ideas (discretionary time) or to address issues and demands from subordinates (subordinate-imposed time).

You want to increase discretionary time, decrease time imposed by superiors and the control system, and do away with time imposed by subordinates.

Time Management Abilities Enhances:

- Good organising
- Appropriate assignment of tasks
- Establishing priorities
- SMART goal formulation
- Control of stress
- Concentrating on just one speciality at a time

PROBLEMS IT SOLVES:

- Poor scheduling
- Taking on multiple tasks at once

HOW TO USE "WHO'S GOT THE MONKEY"

- Identify and characterize the "monkey"; elaborate on the nature of the assignment and the steps required to do it.
- Assign the "monkey" to a specific individual.
- Get the "monkey" insured. Verify that the individual is handling the "monkey" correctly:
    - 01. If a monkey is significant and does not permit errors, you should advise what should be done and take necessary action.
    - 02. If you are confident that the person given the monkey can manage it, take action before offering guidance.

Keeping an eye on the "monkey." Indicate when you'll check in with the monkey to ensure everything proceeds as planned.

ADVANTAGES OF WHO HAS THE MONKEY

- Supervisors can manage their time well.

- Employee problem-solving becomes simpler.
- Equips a precise picture of who is reliable for what.
- A precise method for assigning work.

DISADVANTAGES OF WHO'S GOT MONKEY

- Solely addresses management and work delegation; for excellent overall productivity results, integrate with additional time management techniques.

9. METHOD OF ACTION

The Action Method is predicated on the idea that everything is a project. You interpret, analyze, and manage all of your actions as projects. These initiatives could be:

- Taking care of your money
- Work in administration
- Linked In
- Anything you desire

Time Management Abilities Enhances:

- Planning well and creating SMART goals

PROBLEMS IT SOLVES:

- Poor scheduling
- Taking on multiple tasks at once

HOW ACTION METHOD OPERATES

When you employ the Action Method, you arrange your assignments, events, and activities into projects. Next, you categorize your actions into three groups:

- Steps to Take: These are the things you need to do. These assignments enable you to advance in your work. These include revising a proposal, distributing a completed software, and debugging your most recent app, to name a few.
- References: these consist of summaries, a list of pertinent research links, and outlines to assist you in completing your Action Steps. Put another way, it's everything that acts as a point of reference but doesn't advance you.
- Backburner things are any goals and ideas you have but aren't working on right now but might implement in the future.

ADVANTAGES OF THE ACTION METHOD

- If you approach every everyday task as a project, you'll likely be more organized and practical because each task will have a set of steps.

DISADVANTAGES OF THE ACTION METHOD

- It is time-consuming and possibly overwhelming because you'll have to spend much time preparing if you treat everything as a project.
- There is no timetable for reviewing backlog issues, and it's unclear whether or not you should take on these tasks.

10. THE MATRIX OF EISENHOWER

The Eisenhower Matrix is a time management approach that pertains to prioritizing duties. Its foundation consists in classifying each work as either essential or not necessary or urgent or not urgent.

You prioritize the jobs based on their urgency and importance before beginning work.

The American President Eisenhower, renowned for his efficiency while in office, inspired the naming of the Eisenhower Matrix.

Time Management Abilities Enhances:

- Good organising
- establishing priorities
- focussing on just one thing at a time
- Saying "No"
- Staying away from distractions
- SMART goal formulation
- Appropriate assignment of tasks

PROBLEMS IT SOLVES:

- Poor scheduling
- Deadlines that were missed
- Taking on multiple tasks at once

THE EISENHOWER MATRIX'S OPERATION

Make a list of every task you have and split it into four sections:

- Important and urgent tasks are in the first quadrant. You ought to complete them right away.

- Important but non-urgent tasks are in the second quadrant. When you take them on, you ought to have a plan.
- The third quadrant consists of critical but insignificant tasks. It is best to allot these responsibilities to your coworkers.
- Unimportant and non-urgent tasks are located in the fourth quadrant. They ought to be removed from your itinerary.

ADVANTAGES OF EISENHOWER MATRIX

- A simple rule for setting work priorities.
- Let you think about what you can assign or get rid of.

DISADVANTAGES OF EISENHOWER MATRIX

- Determining the relevance and degree of urgency of assignments could be challenging.
- You could find it difficult to fully apply this strategy due to present bias because you'll be tempted to concentrate on urgent but unimportant chores.

Part 3

Productivity and Time Management

"The key is not to prioritize what's on your schedule but to schedule your priorities."

Stephen Covey

Chapter 5

Maximizing Productivity

Productivity is defined as the capacity to carry out tasks effectively and efficiently. It has nothing to do with how many hours you spend on anything. Being successful and efficient in our professions is what productivity is all about. The amount of work completed in those hours matters more than the number of hours you invest in anything.

To be productive means to complete your job quickly and skillfully. You can spend some time doing something you love by doing this. That is why we all want to be as productive as possible.

One of the significant problems you will face in life is increasing your productivity. For individuals who are currently quite productive, adding more work may seem unnecessary. If you are not doing much, getting started can seem like a tremendous task.

We can adopt several valuable routines, instruments, and practices to simplify our lives and increase productivity in all spheres of life.

We may increase productivity in all our lives by using a few beneficial routines, instruments, and practices.

Determining Peak Productive Times

It's a fact that life is hectic. We have a lot of responsibilities and goals that we need to balance. We also have difficulty finding time for self-care, family vacations, and professional development. Time management has, therefore, become increasingly important in today's world.

Most self-help books and podcasts have tried to convince us that to succeed, we should get up early—ideally around five in the morning—and make the most of our morning hours by working hard and being productive. This schedule isn't ideal for night owls, which work best in the late hours of the day, but it can work for early risers, who give their best work in the morning.

An increasing amount of studies have demonstrated that, with the correct resources, it is possible to modify one's circadian rhythm to more efficiently and naturally wake up in the morning and remain more attentive and focused during the first few hours of the day.

Even while it is possible to change your circadian cycles for sleeping and waking, it won't change the reality that some people are inherently wired to work best in the morning and others in the evening.

Finding your "peak productivity time" of the day can be helpful in this situation. Your "Peak Productivity Time" (abbreviated PPT for simplicity's sake) is the time of day when you feel most focused and driven and when your attention and concentration levels are at their highest.
You may also see from your PowerPoint whether you're a morning or evening person. Finding your PPT will primarily enable you to plan your day so that it naturally serves your needs rather than those of others.

Utilize your PPT time to do the day's most crucial, high-value tasks to perform and execute at your top levels. During our PPT time, we should carefully plan our most mentally taxing significant chores and save the others for times of the day when we're not as alert.

Have you ever pondered when you're most effective at work? Or have you ever asked yourself, "What did I accomplish today?" at the end of the day?

It is not unusual for people to have inconsistent energy levels and different times of productivity throughout the day. While some of us are "morning larks," whose most productive work hours are early in the day, others are "night owls" staying late to work.

Seeing the difference in your performance level will be made easier if you have a clear grasp of when you are most productive and match priority jobs accordingly. We'll go over several easy methods for determining your peak productivity times (PPT) in this section.

1. **Adopt a systematic approach:**

A rigorous approach will help you pinpoint your peak productivity hours more accurately than just going with your intuition.

2. **Record your activity logs in a journal:**

One practical technique to determine whether or not you are spending your time on things that satisfy business objectives is to keep a log of your daily activities. Activity logs can help you discover when you are most productive and can help you schedule high-priority work for the most productive times of the day.

For example, you may spend far more time on social media or taking breaks than you realize. Observing your everyday activities will help determine how much time you spend on specific jobs and activities. From there, you can adjust your work style or cease wasting time on things that won't help you succeed.

This can be accomplished by recording and keeping track of important metrics like;

- Start and finish times for tasks
- How much time you can spend concentrating on a specific task
- How frequently do you get sidetracked at work?
- When are you itching to take a vacation?

You can do this for around a week or a month. After you've collected enough information, examine your work habits and the times when you could concentrate for extended periods. This will allow you to determine when you are most productive and use that time to finish significant assignments requiring precise judgement calls or analytical thought processes.

3. **Check your level of energy:**

The majority of us have regular daily schedules that include getting up in the morning, going to work from 9 to 5, and then relaxing in the evenings. We are supposed to be alert and productive, particularly during working hours. On the other hand, many of us deal with low energy, which causes disruptions in workflow, a lack of desire, and a decline in productivity. Instead, you'll quickly notice that your workflow improves, and you can do more at a reasonable time when you pay attention to and operate in sync with your energy level.

To gauge your energy level and determine when you are most productive, try the following:

- Track your energy levels all day long.
- Record the duration of your moments of high and low energy throughout the day.
- Make an effort to manage your energy and schedule your day appropriately.

This allows you to relocate regular or lower-priority work to places with lower energy and assign critical jobs to areas where you exhibit vital energy.

4. Utilize time-tracking applications:

Ineffective time management is the cause of running out of time on a tight deadline. You may notice that you are taking longer breaks or remaining still or inactive for more extended periods more frequently than not. To get around this, you can install time monitoring software that can keep track of your neutral, productive, and idle hours and provide you with comprehensive analytical productivity reports that you can use for more analysis.

You (or your staff) can take charge of the workload and monitor in real time how quickly you finish a task compared to the day before, thanks to the analysis.

In summary

Ultimately, there is no "one size fits all" solution for maximizing productivity and determining peak hours for productivity. It is vital to regularly test a plan and assess the results to ascertain its effectiveness. It's possible that something that suits someone else won't suit you.

However, by considering your resources, duties, and goals, you can select the best pattern for your optimum productivity. You can maximize your time by selecting tasks and pursuits that yield the most significant benefit and productivity. Finding and utilizing your peak productivity periods can enable you to accomplish more, manage your time more effectively, and achieve more success.

Eliminating Distraction

Gaining the capacity to ignore other distractions and concentrate on your most critical tasks is a crucial skill for any leader or business owner to have.

Your capacity to avoid distractions and maintain attention is a critical component in determining how productive your day will be.

The distractions that are all around you won't go away. If anything, you'll encounter more and more diversions.

One of the best things you can do for yourself if you want to accomplish your goals is to learn how to get over distractions.

It's critical to complete your most important tasks each day, and maintaining focus is necessary to remain productive.

If you are unaware you are distracted, you cannot overcome it. You can implement a strategy to eliminate your distractions once you've determined what's causing them. You may overcome distractions and complete your most critical tasks daily with deliberate time management and good preparation.

Seven (7) Tried-and-True Methods for Reducing Diversion. Utilize these 7 tried-and-true methods to get over distractions.

1. Create a space free from distractions

Distractions immediately apparent to you should be eliminated because many are vying for your attention. When your workstation is messy or disorganized, or when your mind is overly busy, it's simple to become sidetracked.

It's simple to become sidetracked when notifications keep appearing while attempting to concentrate. To enhance your focus, identify the distractions that cause you the most and work through them individually.

2. **Block out time to prevent distractions.**
Switching between tasks can lead to distractions easily. Focusing your attention on a single task is essential to overcoming distractions.

It needs focused time to complete anything meaningful, so schedule a vital activity and set aside time to work on it. Decide exactly what outcome you want, then give yourself a deadline to meet that goal.

When you can concentrate on one item and give it your whole attention, staying focused is made easy.

3. **Take frequent pauses to improve concentration**
Taking regular breaks is crucial to avoiding distractions and maintaining focus. You need to

take breaks to keep your energy and motivation levels if you want to produce more significant and better results.

You can stay focused and produce more when you take regular breaks. By taking breaks, you may ensure you're not sidetracked from your most crucial tasks.

4. Establish daily objectives

Set everyday objectives to help you stay focused and avoid distractions. Keeping your day limited to the essentials will help you avoid becoming sidetracked when you have a lot going on.

To assist you in focusing, you can divide those daily objectives into more minor chores. Reaching a limited amount of daily objectives increases motivation and guarantees you close the day feeling like you've made progress.

5. Give up the habit of being distracted

Start forming routines that support you in removing distractions and guaranteeing your focus to overcome your distracting behaviors.

Examine the routines you follow that lead to feelings of distraction. Next, begin removing each distraction one at a time. This could require arriving at work one hour early, having a break for lunch, and exercising or meditating throughout the day.

Although it may seem easy to change habits, doing so requires dedication. However, a single change could have a transformative effect.

6. Maintain a deliberate focus

If you want to stop being distracted, you need to start being deliberate in everything you do. When you are intentional, you know your goals in every circumstance.

Since you've already determined what you want to do, being intentional helps you stay focused. Focus is improved, and distractions are eliminated when one is purposeful.

7. Make a detailed plan for the day.

Without a defined plan for the day, it's easy to become sidetracked. Make preparation an integral element of your workday to combat distractions.

To ensure you know exactly where to spend your time on Monday morning, schedule your week on a Friday or Sunday.

This guarantees you won't go sidetracked at the beginning of the week.

To ensure that you begin the day with complete focus, plan your day the night before. To ensure your day is productive, list the three tasks you wish to do.

In Conclusion

With everything going on at work, it's simple to become sidetracked. Try some of these strategies to avoid distractions and maintain your attention.

You can be more productive at work and finish larger, better projects faster without distractions.

Why is it crucial to get rid of distractions?

Distractions might make you feel stressed and anxious, particularly if you're pressed for time or have a backlog of work.

In the modern world, where we are continuously inundated with alerts, messages, and other distractions that can impair our concentration and productivity, learning to reduce distractions is an essential ability.

Distractions can be removed to lower stress levels, make the workspace calmer, focus entirely on the task at hand, and increase the likelihood of finishing it faster.

Techniques of Focus and Concentration

Have you encountered difficulties maintaining focus? To work smarter, not harder, it's critical to learn how to reduce distractions and sharpen your attention in all areas of your life, including business, job, school, and daily life.
People these days seem to be having trouble focusing and feeling overloaded in both their personal and professional lives. It's not your fault, either.

Working remotely or in an office requires balancing many obligations and tasks, which almost always results in overwhelm and forgetfulness.

With so much to comprehend and many distractions, your brain becomes increasingly congested and worn out over the day. Your brain will start to gravitate less toward focused endeavors and more toward distractions as this is happening.

Research indicates that every task you complete tends to reduce your effectiveness at the subsequent work; this is particularly true for high-stakes tasks requiring a high degree of self-control or judgment.

What is meant by Focus?
The ability to focus allows you to pay attention to the task at hand. Distractions are reduced, and productivity is boosted. You won't have to work as hard to concentrate on the task at hand when you're feeling focused. During times of focus, your mind could feel clearer, which might help you stay engrossed in what matters to you at that particular moment.

The mental effort you put into whatever you're working on or learning at the time is called concentration. Although attention and focus span are sometimes used interchangeably, focus span describes how long you can focus on something.

What is meant by Concentration?
It is a talent that may be mastered with patience and effort. Thus, try not to be too hard on yourself

the next time you catch yourself daydreaming. Acknowledge it, refocus, and acknowledge the little triumphs of focused attention.

How to Sharpen your Concentration and Focus: Eight methods for concentration and focus

1. **Eliminate distractions to establish a space free from them.**

Make your surroundings as distraction-free as you can to start. Put your phone on silent and tidy up your desk. Make sure it's only you when it's time to concentrate

2. **Take one task at a time.**

Although multitasking can make you feel busy, it impairs your ability to concentrate. Alternatively, focus on only one task at a time. Before going on to the next task, complete the one you started.

Overcommitting to a task can be mentally taxing. Try to settle down by focusing on one task at a time.

3. **Practice mindfulness to sharpen your concentration skills.**

Every day, set aside a short period to practice meditation and mindfulness. Your ability to concentrate when it matters most can be enhanced by these techniques, which teach your brain to focus on the here and now. Examining the exercises on the Calm app can be an excellent place to start if you're new to mindfulness.

4. Make getting enough sleep a priority to maintain focus.

Sleep for 7 to 9 hours every night. Well-rested brains are sharper and more efficient. If you have trouble falling asleep, try using some sleep noises or working on techniques to help your mind unwind before bed.

5. Don't stress about the next duty; instead, stay in the present.

Stay in the moment. Remember where your body is at all times. Keep your attention on the task and gently refocus your thoughts when they stray.

6. Divide up your work or projects to refuel your mind.

To help you regain your attention span, work for shorter periods and then take a quick rest. Put the Pomodoro Technique to Use: Work for 25 minutes, then take a 5-minute rest. Labor.

7. Walk outside to clear your head

To help your brain relax, have a connection with nature. Spending a short while outside can help you focus and clear your head.

8. To help you stay focused, keep moving.

Frequent exercise has benefits beyond physical health. It also does wonders for your brain. Your brain receives oxygen when you exercise, which improves focus. Thus, your brain will appreciate you if you stroll, work out, or stretch.

Three types of focus

- **Inward Focus**

Is the process of tuning into your emotions and thoughts to have a deeper understanding of who you are. Sorting through your ideas and staying focused is much easier when you are conscious of what's going on inside your mind.

- **External Focus**

Entails having awareness of your surroundings. Your ability to observe details and comprehend the overall structure of your surroundings is enhanced by outer focus. This could be listening intently when someone is speaking to you, observing a shift in the weather, or even just keeping track of your keys.

- **Different Focus**

Is focused on individuals besides oneself. It's the kind of concentration you employ when you listen to a friend, try to understand their feelings, or collaborate with others to complete a task.

Everyone experiences times of distraction; these might be caused by fatigue, being in a noisy environment, or simply having a lot on their mind. That is entirely typical. The secret is to be able to spot when your attention is straying and quickly return it to the proper place.

Advantages of Maintaining Concentration

Maintaining focus on a primary task can have tremendous advantages in the business. Whatever your field, honing your focus and concentration skills will help you succeed professionally. The following four advantages of maintaining focus during work:

A. Increases vigor

You're more likely to finish a job quickly when you focus on it. Your ability to complete assignments more quickly may inspire you to go on to the next. Your confidence in completing tasks will keep you upbeat and encourage you to reach your next objective.

B. Boosts output

You'll be able to finish more things overall the more you can maintain focus. Reducing outside distractions is an excellent approach to maintain focus and give your brain time to absorb what has to be done. Concentrating your concentration in one area will likely help you as a working professional complete more tasks.

C. Lowers tension

Tension and pressure will be reduced due to staying focused and working more productively. You may cross more tasks off your to-do list and gain more time in your work schedule when concentrating on a single activity. Your ability to focus your efforts will ensure you don't procrastinate or scramble to fulfill deadlines.

D. Generates higher-quality work

Your performance at work depends heavily on your capacity for concentration. Your ability to focus and dedicate more time to a task will result in higher-quality output. You'll not only finish assignments more quickly, but you'll also make sure they are error-free.

Why you could be having trouble focusing
It may be an indication to check in with yourself and pay attention to your body's signals if you lose focus. There are several possible causes for your inability to maintain concentration. These are a handful:

- **Weary:** To focus, your brain needs energy. It may be difficult for you to focus on the current task if you are fatigued.

- Not getting enough sleep can cause your thoughts to wander more because sleep is like recharging your brain's battery.
- An excessive amount of stress might make it difficult to concentrate on anything else. Your mind is preoccupied with wondering about the source of your stress.

- Absence of exercise Frequent movement improves focus by boosting blood flow to the brain. Your brain may have difficulty staying focused if you're not moving around frequently.

- **Dietary decisions:** Your ability to concentrate might be affected by hunger and thirst, but your diet can also have an impact. Certain foods may provide a short-lived energy spike, but they may also create an energy slump that causes you to lose focus. Different nutrients, such as fruits, vegetables, and whole grains, can assist your focus more effectively.

You can learn which foods improve your ability to focus and which ones don't by engaging in Mindful Eating practices.

Circumstances that impact the Focus

Difficulties focusing can be related to external events. Social media notifications, coworker interruptions, and diversions from family members or roommates are common culprits.

However, there's also a chance that underlying mental or physical health issues are connected to concentration issues. Typical ones are as follows:

- Attention-deficit/hyperactivity disorder, or ADHD, can cause problems with memory and learning in both adults and children. Usually, impulsivity, hyperactivity, and persistent patterns of inattention are what define ADHD. ADHD symptoms may improve with treatment.

- Concentration, memory, and learning can all be impacted by cognitive dysfunction or disability. These difficulties may include neurological disorders that impair brain function, developmental delays or disabilities, or brain injuries.

- The main indications of untreated mental health issues like anxiety or depression include mood swings and other emotional signs. However, they can also make it difficult to concentrate, focus, or pick up and retain new knowledge. Stress may also make it more difficult to concentrate at work or school.

- Concussions and other head trauma can impact memory loss and concentration. Until this is usually very temporary, focus issues can persist until a concussion heals.

- Attention and concentration issues can be brought on by farsightedness and other visual problems. You might wish to have your eyes examined if you (or your child) are experiencing headaches, squinting, or difficulty concentrating.

- Your ability to focus can be affected by distractions like social media, incoming calls, and a bustling atmosphere. Try turning off electronics and finding a neat area with less traffic and noise if you want to focus.
- Lack of sleep might impair one's ability to focus. Maintain a healthy sleep schedule by, among other things, leaving electronics outside your room and trying to go to bed and wake up at the same time every day.

- Drinking alcohol can impair your cognitive function. The brain is where alcohol goes first after consumption, and it can have an impact on your capacity to concentrate, think clearly, make judgments, control your words and conduct, and so on.

- Certain medications, especially those used to treat high blood pressure, can occasionally cause brain fog. See if any medications may make you sleepy or have any other side effects on your brain by reading the material that comes with them.

It takes time to increase focus and concentration. Gaining more clarity in your focus and capacity to concentrate takes time. Professional athletes, such as sprinters, gymnasts, and golfers, prepare for a long time and are typically coached to focus and execute their moves flawlessly.

Realizing how your lack of concentration impacts your life is the first step towards improving it. It's time to get help with concentration so that you can concentrate on what matters most to you if you are finding it challenging to keep your promises, always getting sidetracked by little things, or failing to make headway on your objectives.

Success in your job and personal life depends on your ability to focus while working. You'll discover that you can do more things you value and feel better about yourself when you focus better. To live a meaningful and fulfilling life, it's important to prioritize creating time for joy and happiness and completing duties.

Chapter 6

Time Management Skills

Have you ever wondered why some people always appear to be racing from one task to the next and never seem to finish anything, while others seem to have enough time to do all they want to?

It can't be that some folks only have less work to accomplish. There's a significantly higher probability that they are managing their time well or employing it more efficiently.

Persuasive time management is an important proficient skill to master. Keeping your daily duties organized can help you prioritize your projects, finish work on schedule, and update coworkers and superiors on your progress. Attaining important objectives and growing professionally can eventually result from having excellent time management abilities. We'll discuss identifying and ranking tasks in this part to get the best outcomes.

Having Limits and Refusing Requests

We frequently juggle several obligations and responsibilities in today's fast-paced society, leaving little time for ourselves. Saying yes to everything while ignoring our own needs is an easy trap to get into. But this never-ending giving without a vacation might harm our emotional and physical health. Because of this, it's crucial to set limits and say no to preserve a positive work-life balance and safeguard our mental health.

We will discuss the significance of establishing boundaries and saying no to our mental health in this part. We'll discuss the detrimental effects of not setting limits on our mental health and offer helpful advice on how to create sound boundaries and feel confident in saying no when it's essential.

We hope this article gives you essential insights into the advantages of creating boundaries and gives you the confidence to put your mental health first, regardless of whether you're a people-pleaser or find it challenging to prioritize your needs.

What do boundaries mean?

Personal constraints that specify what we are and are not ready to accept are called boundaries. They safeguard our mental and physical well-being by establishing boundaries for our emotional and physical space. Setting limits can take many forms, such as refusing excessive requests, avoiding harmful relationships, or scheduling self-care time. Boundaries essentially assist us in striking a healthy balance between our requirements as individuals and those of the outside world.

Why do boundaries matter?
Setting and establishing boundaries is crucial to living a happy and healthy existence. They safeguard our mental health and wellness, assist us in forming and preserving wholesome connections, and keep us from becoming burned out or resentful. Without boundaries, we could experience feelings of being overburdened, agitated, exploited, and unable to allocate our time and exertion efficiently.

By establishing boundaries, we can safeguard our time and energy, prioritize our needs, and establish a positive balance that enhances our general well-being.

They assist us in communicating to others what we deem appropriate or inappropriate, as well as how we should assertively, but non-aggressively, communicate our requirements. Individuals who have firm boundaries typically experience less stress and have greater self-esteem.

The Advantages of Establishing Boundaries
The following are some advantages of establishing boundaries in your life:
- Safeguarding your well-being and mental health.
- Fostering wholesome relationships by setting boundaries and expectations that are clear.
- Setting your needs and time first will help you avoid burnout and tiredness.
- Appreciating your time and effort to improve your sense of self-worth and dignity.
- Communicating your wants and limitations to others will help you become a better communicator.
- Focused on critical activities and removing distractions to increase productivity.
- Lowering tension and anxiety by staying away from pointless obligations.

- Fostering personal development by scheduling time for introspection and self-care.
- Improving your feeling of independence and control over your life.
- Encouraging a positive work-life balance that is beneficial to your general well-being.
- Having friends and family understand and accept you.

Instances of Establishing Boundaries

A boundary could be as simple as telling someone to behave differently, such as "I prefer calm conversations. Please stop yelling at me."

It can also be something we do for our safety, like banning someone's number, getting out of a room if it bothers us, or setting limits on our privacy and personal space with family and friends.

Saying no to social gatherings or obligations that conflict with your beliefs or interests, as well as minimizing the amount of time you spend with negative individuals or those who drain your energy, are examples of personal boundaries.

Our professional life also has boundaries. Work boundaries could be as simple as setting up specific work hours, refraining from working on job-related chores during downtime, and saying no to irrational demands or requests beyond your capacity or availability. This is another way to set boundaries, whether they are in your personal or professional life.

It is setting aside time for self-care and giving pursuits that advance your well-being as a top priority.

Setting and maintaining boundaries enables us to be honest about our expectations and to treat others and ourselves with respect.

What may we Impose Boundaries on?
- Momentum
- Individual room
- Sexuality
- Feeling power
- Social networks
- financial resources or material belongings
- Ethics and morals

How can we Establish Healthy Boundaries?

It might not be easy to set appropriate boundaries, particularly if you're accustomed to prioritizing the needs of others over your own. But you can learn to set and uphold appropriate boundaries that promote your welfare if you put in the time and effort.

Establishing your needs and priorities, communicating effectively and assertively, learning when to say no, avoiding people and situations that deplete your energy, putting self-care first, and asking for help when required are some strategies for setting good boundaries. It's critical to remember that establishing boundaries is an essential part of living a happy and healthy life, not a sign of selfishness.

Face Your Fear of Limiting Yourself and Saying No

General fear gets in the way of your desire to say no. You can overcome your fear if you deal with it. False Evidence Appearing Real, or FEAR, is a beautiful acronym used in 12-step programs. It indicates that most of the time, our fears are unfounded.

Ask yourself, "What is your biggest fear when it comes to turning down an invitation?" as you consider these anxieties. Do you think they'll go because they're angry with you, for instance? Do you believe they'll perceive you as being self-centered?

After you've given a name to that dread, consider the likelihood that it will materialize. What does that indicate about the person you're associated with if it did happen? Acknowledging your needs shouldn't be seen negatively.

When we start imposing limits and saying no, some people don't like it, but they will probably learn to appreciate you for it. It could be time to reevaluate the relationship if they cannot accept you saying no. When something doesn't work for them, everyone is free to opt-out.

We teach others how to treat us when we don't establish appropriate limits. When boundaries are absent, relationships deteriorate. Relationships become obligations when one party contributes more than the other and can even approach codependency.

When Creating Boundaries Modifies Your Inner Dialogue!

Take into account your inner dialogue when establishing boundaries. Is your "self-talk" or internal conversion informing you that people will be upset if you refuse?

You are imagining the worst—false evidence that seems genuine. Change your "self-talk" to more upbeat, practical statements instead. You tell yourself things like, "You can do this," or "It's okay to have needs," to maintain a positive outlook.

Indices of Sound Boundaries
- You don't feel bad for declining.
- You refuse to be used or abused by others.
- You can resist under duress.
- The boundaries set by others don't bother you.
- You don't think you have to take care of other adults.
- You don't take offense at the criticism of others.
- You accept accountability for your triggers.
- You honor the limits set by others.
- You respect your emotions and rights.
- Others don't have to concur with you.
- What happens if we lack sound boundaries?

Without boundaries, we risk feeling overburdened, tense, and worn out, resulting in burnout and possibly physical health issues. We might also experience low self-esteem and have trouble expressing our needs and boundaries to others, which can strain our relationships and cause further stress.

We can believe that voicing our demands is wrong and self-serving if we don't have healthy boundaries. Ineffective boundaries increase the likelihood that we will be taken advantage of and wind up in toxic relationships with friends, family, lovers, and coworkers. Setting good boundaries can cause some discomfort, so we need to learn to expect this and learn to live with it.

When we don't establish appropriate boundaries as adults, we run the risk of entering into toxic relationships that can result in abuse, manipulation, and resentment.

We risk losing our pleasure and well-being to satisfy the demands and expectations of others if we don't prioritize self-care and set boundaries. It is crucial to acknowledge the advantages of establishing sound limits and to create and uphold them in our day-to-day existence proactively.

It requires skill to establish boundaries. Seeking support from a highly valued someone may be beneficial if you are experiencing suicidal thoughts as a result of struggling to recognize your boundaries. This can help you decompress and feel better about yourself by giving you the time and space to consider how healthy your boundaries are, how to say no, and how to reduce stress.

Making Use of Technological Tools to Manage Time

Technology can help you become more productive and maintain focus. Think about how long it used to take to send a message via the mail instead of how instantaneous email is nowadays. But while you look into how technology affects time management, you must also consider ensuring technology doesn't get in the way of your goals. You can use the technology in conjunction with an online time duration calculator. Indeed, what if you could do your responsibilities on time? A clock calculator can help you with that.

The internet era and technology are frequently criticized for being time wasters that lower quality of life and productivity. To be sure, it is not unusual to work on a subject that started as a focused, particular, and time-bound undertaking, only to find yourself lost in a maze of hyperlinks and distractions.

The misconception that multitasking is a "superpower" of the digital age is closely related to distractions, ineffective time management, and decreased productivity. However, you may monitor the output with a time calculator.

Research has shown that digital natives have a lower emotional engagement in any given activity because they switch between several digital media platforms roughly once each minute. This is the most typical explanation for ineffective time management. However, an online time calculator could be a simple tool to help with time management. To guarantee project completion, businesses rely on computer systems and the cloud.

In addition, internet calendars have replaced paper to-do lists. The ability of technology to save time and effort is its primary function. Tools with a vital technological component that save you a lot of time also increase productivity and efficiency in general. Thus, it is possible to say that technology and time management go hand in hand. You will discover how technology affects time management in this post.

1. **Utilize Technology to Make Your Daily Schedule**

Making a detailed schedule for your day is a great way to manage your time. How often have we questioned where the day has gone as the end of the day comes? Making a plan for your day's activities will help prevent it from passing you by. We can get help from technology in this area. Online calendars help us plan our events and serve as a reminder so we don't forget them. You may even synchronize these calendars with your mobile device. Additionally, a time duration calculator may allow you to lower the time hazards associated with completing specific jobs.

Many of the web calendars we use today are integrated right into our email clients. It can take a little while to become familiar with your program's capabilities and how to take advantage of them. Once again, calendars and scheduling tools must be inconspicuous and easy to use. You won't use them if they aren't since they take up more time than they save.

For groups, online calendars can be a beneficial time management tool. It can help to prevent needless disruptions to know when significant activities are scheduled for your team members. Additionally, it can help plan meetings and other activities for groups. Calculators for time duration can also help you schedule meetings at the appropriate times.

Making the most of any scheduling program requires proper training, particularly if you plan to use it with a group of people. Teach group members how to operate the technology for a while. Establish some fundamental guidelines for the group's use of the technology so that everyone is aware of its importance.

Taking charge of your schedule is an essential first step in creating a time management plan. After that, all you need to do is choose the appropriate tools to help you maximize your 24-hour day. Try out different technologies without fear to find the one that suits you best.

2. **Modifying Business Communication**

The fact that technology has altered communication norms is one of its many advantages. Chat apps, social networking sites, and smartphones offer a successful new method of communication. Different degrees of communication have been established and have been quite successful. You can now speak with coworkers, instructors, and friends without issues.

You can communicate by text, video, or email with coworkers or superiors using social networking apps like Skype, WhatsApp, and others. You can even hold video conferences with these apps. With technology, you may stay in touch with your company or business without being physically there.

One of the most significant developments in technology to date is this. Using conference calls and video chats, you may continue communicating with your coworkers while working on other crucial projects away from the office. To ensure that you do not struggle to finish your work, a time duration calculator can also help you manage the duration of your online video calls.

3. Maintain A Completely Organized Schedule

Technology helps with corporate organization. One technological solution that can help you keep your everyday tasks completely organized is project management software. The date interval calculator is a valuable tool as well. It's easy for managers and employers to keep an eye on employee activity, which helps to keep things moving forward. It demonstrates accountability, responsibility, effectiveness, and punctuality in completing the tasks given to each individual.

Today's modern workplace offers many cutting-edge tools and software to boost productivity. Project management software not only dictates the repercussions of poor decisions but also helps increase the number and quality of work produced. It motivates us to use technology to improve living conditions globally. It is the source of our promising future and aids in organizing everything.

4. Utilizing Various Apps for Your Work

Many software are available for organizing tasks and to-do lists. One such tool that is accessible is an online time calculator. Try it if you currently use Google Drive and other Google productivity products. Although it is a small application, its easy-to-use interface makes it a valuable tool when used with other programs.

Thankfully, many technical solutions are available to support your more effective and efficient planning, prioritization, and work execution. In this paragraph, we'll look at some of the top technological tools for time management and how to get the most out of them.

- **Calendar Software**

Calendar software is among the most fundamental time management tools. Using a calendar app, you can arrange your appointments, activities, meetings, and deadlines in one location and synchronize them across all your platforms and devices. To stay on course and not miss or forget anything crucial, you can also create alerts, notifications, and reminders.

Additionally, calendar software may assist you in scheduling time for your personal interests, projects, and responsibilities and create a flexible and realistic daily, weekly, or monthly schedule. Calendar, Apple Calendar, Google Calendar, and Outlook are a few of the most widely used calendar software.

- **Managers of tasks**

A task manager is an additional tool that can assist you in improving your time management. An app or piece of software called a task manager aids in the planning, monitoring, and completing your tasks and subtasks. Tasks can be organized into lists, categories, labels, and tags using a task manager. You can assign tasks dependencies, priorities, due dates, and statuses. A task manager can also assign assignments to people, work together as a team, and keep track of your performance and advancement. You may focus on the most crucial and pressing activities, break down your goals into manageable steps, and prevent overwhelm and procrastination using a task manager. The most widely used task managers are Wunderlist, Asana, Trello, and Todoist.

- **Time-keeping devices**

One tool that can assist you in tracking the amount of time you spend on jobs, activities, and projects is a time tracker. Using a time tracker can assist you in determining how you spend your time, where you squander it, and how to become more proficient at managing your time. With a time tracker, you can record your start and end times, set timers, and create reports and charts that display your production and efficiency and your time distribution. You can assess your workload, set reasonable expectations, and accurately bill your clients with a time tracker. The most well-known time trackers are Clockify, Harvest, Toggl, and RescueTime.

- **Timer Pomodoros**

You can utilize the Pomodoro technique, a time management strategy that involves working in brief, concentrated spurts interspersed with short pauses, with a Pomodoro timer. You may lessen your weariness, tension, and distractions while also improving your motivation, creativity, and concentration using the Pomodoro technique. You can break up your work into 25-minute blocks, or Pomodoros, and take 5-minute breaks in between by using a Pomodoro timer. A more extended rest lasting fifteen to thirty minutes is taken after every four Pomodoros. To keep track of the Pomodoros you've accomplished, analyze your performance, and modify your strategy as necessary, you can also use a Pomodoro timer. Tomato Timer, Focus Booster, PomoDone, and Marinara Timer are a few of the most well-liked Pomodoro timers.

- **Distraction Blockers**

Distraction blockers are tools that assist you in reducing or getting rid of distractions that get in the way of your productivity and time management. You can restrict or block access to websites, apps, social media, games, and other online temptations that take your focus away from your work with a distraction blocker.

Distraction blockers can also be used to silence or stop emails, calls, texts, and notifications that obstruct your concentration. With a distraction blocker, you can improve your work environment, become more disciplined and strong-willed, and do more tasks in less time. Distraction blockers like Freedom, StayFocusd, Cold Turkey, and Forest are some of the most often used ones.

What else do you think about this?
Examples, tales, or thoughts that don't fit into the other parts can be shared here. What more are you willing to say?

Part 4

Overcoming Challenges

"Success is not final, failure is not fatal: It is the courage to continue that counts."

Winston Churchill

Chapter 7

Building Resilience

We all face challenging and unforeseen situations in life. Being resilient is an essential characteristic that can help us deal with life's unpredictability and prosper in the face of hardship.

Understanding and developing resilience can influence the way we face life's challenges, whether they are related to managing daily stressors at work, significant life changes, or everyday obstacles. It can provide us with the inner fortitude to overcome the barriers, adjust to change, and carry on forward.

What is meant by Resilience?

Our capacity to bounce back from adversity is resilience. It enables us to take on life's obstacles head-on and come out stronger and wiser in the process. Put another way, it has to do with growth and adaptation. Being resilient in the face of unforeseen events entails accepting the challenges, changing course, drawing lessons from them, and coming up with constructive solutions to carry on with a fresh sense of purpose.

Even under extreme stress, resilient people seek out answers, rely on their networks of support, and maintain their optimism. Over time, everyone may learn and become more resilient, and every setback presents a chance for personal development.

The ability to bounce back from setbacks, ask for assistance when things become too much to handle, and persevere in the face of setbacks are all signs of resilience. Having a resilient mindset gives you the ability to face life's ups and downs with grit and grace.

Typical Obstacles to Resilience

It's not always easy to develop resilience, and some events can make it more challenging. Fortunately, being aware of the difficulties posed by each obstacle will enable you to locate solutions and assistance to go past them.

- **Chronic health problems:** It's critical to acknowledge the additional difficulties that chronic physical or mental health disorders bring since they have the potential to sap

resilience. Seek advice from medical professionals to successfully manage your disease, and look for support groups to connect with people going through similar struggles.
- **Prejudice:** Being the target of prejudice can seriously hinder resilience. Look for groups and mentors who may offer consolation and helpful guidance.
- **Tense relationships:** Your resilience may be impacted by tense interactions with family or friends. Initiate a conversation with the individuals concerned, or look for advice from a mediator or counselor; they can assist you in managing or mending these connections while strengthening your emotional bond.
- **Loneliness:** Being alone can prevent the development of resilience. To start making new friends, consider joining online forums or community groups that share your interests.
- **Financial hardships:** Money-related stress can be a significant obstacle to resilience. For advice on handling financial difficulties, look into local resources or financial counseling programs.

- **Service accessibility:** Resilience may be impacted by restricted access to vital services like healthcare and education. Look for regional associations or government initiatives that offer assistance in these fields.
- **Single parents:** Raising a child alone presents difficulties that may weaken resilience. It can be pretty beneficial to establish a support network through local or online support groups where you can exchange stories and guidance.
- **Caregivers:** Developing resilience can be challenging because providing care can be draining. Plan frequent pauses and look for respite care to ensure you have time for self-care whenever possible.
- **Living circumstances:** Poor quality housing may make it more difficult for you to cope. Look into any local support services or housing aid programs that might be able to help you get a better place to live.

The 7 C's of Resilience

While each person's road toward developing greater resilience is unique, several traits can support you. You can build a solid foundation for navigating challenging circumstances by comprehending and practicing the Seven C's of resilience.

1. Proficiency
Being competent entails being ready for and able to manage challenging circumstances. You can overcome obstacles by applying your knowledge when a problem emerges and facing difficulties efficiently.

2. Self-assurance
Being confident involves having faith in your abilities and judgment, especially when things are difficult. Being confident doesn't imply you won't ever experience uncertainty or fear; instead, you know you can get through these emotions.

3. Establishment of Connection
Resilience depends on having healthy, supportive connections. Relationships with coworkers, family, and friends can help you get support and guidance when needed. When times are hard, they can offer support and direction while reassuring you that you're not alone.

4. Personality
Knowing who you are and upholding your morals and beliefs under duress are qualities that define

character. It entails deciding what's ideal for you by comprehending the distinction between positive and wrong and what it implies. In the face of difficulty, those with strong moral integrity are frequently seen as dependable and trustworthy.

5. Input
Having a constructive influence on the environment can significantly increase resilience. Engaging in acts of kindness, financial donations, or volunteer work can all contribute to a sense of purpose and community. Having a sense of accomplishment can be empowering when things are hard.

6. Coping
Resilience depends on learning constructive coping mechanisms for adversity and stress. Activities like exercise, meditation, talking to friends, or taking up a hobby can all be used as coping mechanisms. You can use these to control your emotions and maintain your composure when things get tough.

7. Mastery
You may focus on the things you can change and let go of the things that are out of your custody when you admit the sites of your life that you can

govern and accept the ones you cannot. This can give you more confidence to take constructive action and lessen emotions of helplessness.

Coping Mechanisms for Failures and Setbacks

Life's unavoidable obstacles—failure and setbacks—shape our path to resilience and personal development. Our response to these situations, whether they involve a lost opportunity, a project that doesn't work out, or an unfulfilled personal goal, can significantly affect our mental and general well-being. The secret to changing our viewpoint and coming out more vital is to accept these experiences as worthwhile teachings rather than overwhelming challenges.

The following are essential ideas for handling failure and setbacks; I came across a few enlightening facts:

1. **Reasons for Setbacks and the Effect of Setbacks:**

- People tend to overlook external causes of failures and instead blame internal ones. The setback effect is the tendency to ignore outside influences, which increases the likelihood of future failures.
- Refocusing on goals and maintaining self-confidence can help people avoid the setback effect. This attitude shift involves concentrating on external factors that led to the failure.

2. **Reaction to Mistakes and Obstacles:**
    - Successful people set themselves apart by how they handle failure, not by the fact that they never fail. This entails reacting with more vigor and a revitalized dedication to objectives instead of losing heart and quitting.
    - It is always better to plan for failures than to try to avoid them, especially if you are a perfectionist or take a strict approach to achieving your goals.

3. **The Right and Wrong Ways to Handle Failure:**

- ➤ DON'T Focus on Past Errors: Depression increases when focusing on past mistakes. Instead, grant yourself forgiveness and go forward.
- ➤ DO Pay Attention to Your Future Objectives: Make the most of setbacks to inspire you to work harder for long-term goals.
- ➤ AVOID Being Avoidant: Refusing to fail can cause anxiety and make it difficult to grow from little setbacks.
- ➤ ACT as a Seeker: Concentrate on potential successes, be open to trying new things and failing forward.
- ➤ DON'T Be a Difficult Sticker: Know when a plan isn't working and be prepared to adjust your strategy.
- ➤ DO Make Quick Adjustments: Reframe failures as failed experiments and concentrate on growing, adapting, and persevering instead of giving up.

Comprehending Setbacks: Beyond Mere Failures

Despite being mistaken for failures, setbacks are stepping stones to achievement. It has been shown by well-known individuals like Thomas Edison and contemporary inventors like Elon Musk that mistakes are only a necessary element of creativity and learning. Edison's journey, which included multiple failed efforts until he ultimately invented the light bulb, is a prime example of the value of tenacity and grit.

Techniques for Overcoming Obstacles

1. Acknowledge your feelings:
It's critical to permit yourself to experience the sensations accompanying failure and disappointment. Suppressing or disregarding your feelings, whether annoyance, rage, or sadness, might exacerbate the circumstance. Recognize your emotions and give yourself time to work through them.

2. Reframe the circumstances:
Try to reframe setbacks and failures as opportunities for progress rather than as the end of the road. Consider how you can use the experience to better yourself and what lessons you can take from it. If you didn't pass an exam, for instance, take that as a chance to figure out your weaknesses and address them going forward.

3. Develop self-compassion:

When we fail or face setbacks, it can be simple to be hard on ourselves, but it's crucial to learn self-compassion. Be kind and understanding to yourself, like a friend going through a difficult moment. Remind yourself that you're not the only one who has disappointments and setbacks in life.

4. **Look for assistance:**
Never hesitate to ask for help from friends, family, or a mental health professional. You can digest your emotions and experiences and obtain fresh insight by discussing them. Furthermore, asking for assistance might make you feel less alone and more a part of the community.

5. **Take action:**
To go forward, you must act even though it's necessary to give yourself time to comprehend setbacks and failures. Make sure your goals are reasonable, and start small to achieve them. Along the journey, acknowledge your accomplishments and remember that failures and setbacks do not mean the end of the trip.

Accepting Difficulties: Developing Resilience and Self-Assurance

It is essential to accept obstacles and grow from them to develop resilience. This is realizing that failures are transitory and concentrating on objectives and accomplishments in the future. It is crucial to understand that failures are a necessary component of learning rather than a reflection of one's shortcomings.

Realistic Methods for Overcoming Obstacles

- **Anticipate and Get Ready for Obstacles:** Recognize that obstacles are a natural part of life and mentally prepare to overcome them.
- **Steer clear of the blame game:** Rather than blaming, concentrate on the lessons that can be drawn from the event.
- **Take Effective Action:** Make the most of failures by utilising them as motivation to work harder and more methodically towards your goals.
- **Seek Assistance When Needed:** Speaking with someone might occasionally offer new insight and much-needed assistance.

It's critical to remember that obstacles are not the end of the road in our quest for self-improvement but rather essential stops along the way. Through adeptly managing these obstacles, we can transform our failures into victories, cultivating an outlook of development and adaptability.

Developing a Positive Attitude Towards Failure

It's essential to learn how to look at setbacks with optimism. It entails not just a mental shift but also doable actions to guarantee that you recover more fully. The following are some tactics to foster this optimistic outlook:

- **Consciously Accepting:** Realize that obstacles are a necessary component of development. By embracing them with awareness, one can stop unpleasant feelings from taking control.
- **Emphasis on Takeaways**: Every failure teaches you something. Determine the lessons you may take away from each encounter to steer clear of the same problems later on.
- **Establish sensible objectives**: Rethink your objectives in light of the failure. Establishing reasonable, attainable goals might aid in confidence restoration.
- **Request Assistance and Input:** Observations from the outside can occasionally yield insightful information. Never be afraid to

ask peers, mentors, or experts for advice or assistance.

The Significance of Self-Compassion in Handling Failures

Having self-compassion is essential when one is experiencing failures. Practice self-compassion instead of critical self-criticism. Recognize that failure and setbacks are a part of life and affect everyone. This method aids in keeping a realistic viewpoint on your experiences.

Practical Strategies for Overcoming Setbacks in Your Personal and Career

1. Adopt a Growth Mindset by viewing obstacles as chances for your growth.
2. **Put Resilience Into Practice**: Resilience can be developed by accepting and growing from setbacks.
3. **Sustain a Support Network**: Be in the company of individuals who inspire and encourage you.
4. **Remain Adaptable and Flexible**: Be flexible and prepared to modify your tactics.

Overcoming Obstacles in the Workplace

Setbacks in the workplace can take many different forms, such as an unsuccessful project, an opportunity for advancement, or even losing your job. Handling issues calls for a combination of emotional intelligence and strategic thinking.

For example, once a project fails, instead of focusing on what went wrong, consider how it could be done better in future endeavors. Use the time you have to upskill or look into new professional prospects if you're adjusting to losing your job.

Critical Strategies for Turning Failure Into Success

Accepting setbacks and failure as necessary for success is crucial for one's development. Focus and strategy are needed to turn these experiences into success tales.

- **Think Back and Reevaluate:** Think about what went wrong and why. This reevaluation approach aids in identifying the underlying reasons behind the setback.
- **Create a Resilience Mentality**: Develop the mentality that failure is just a momentary obstacle that can be overcome. Having this mentality can help you recover more fully.

- **Make a plan of action**: Create a detailed plan of action to proceed. This can entail making new plans, picking up new abilities, or asking for advice.

Handling the Emotional Effects of Failure

Failure and failures can have a profound emotional toll. It is crucial to deal with these emotions positively.

- **Recognize Your Feelings**: Permitting yourself to feel let down is okay, but try not to let these feelings consume you.
- **Get Emotional Assistance**: Speak with loved ones, friends, or experts who can offer emotional support and direction.
- **Practice Self-Care**: Give mental and emotional health-promoting activities a top priority.

Making the Most of Setbacks to Advance Yourself

Setbacks and failures can be effective stimulants for human development. They present chances to grow in knowledge, flexibility, and resilience. Here's how to use failures as opportunities for growth:

1. **Examine Your Experience**: Dissect the event to determine what transpired and why.
2. **Determine Potential for Growth:** Seek opportunities for skill development or areas for improvement.
3. **Apply the Knowledge Gained:** Use the knowledge you learned from failures to guide your future choices and activities.

Overcoming Emotional Reactions to Setbacks and Aggression

When faced with setbacks, emotional emotions like rage or irritation are frequent. Controlling these responses is essential to positively addressing the circumstance.

1. **Identify Triggers:** Recognize the things that set off your emotional responses.
2. **Practice Calmness Techniques**: You can control your aggressive reactions by practicing calm techniques like deep breathing or meditation.
3. **If Needed, Seek Professional Assistance**: If you struggle to control your emotions, you might want help from a professional.

Accepting Failures as Chances

Recall that handling failure and setbacks involves how you react to them rather than trying to prevent them. You can use the appropriate techniques to transform these encounters into chances for achievement and personal development.

Valuable Resources for Overcoming Failure and Setbacks

Effectively managing failure and setbacks calls for valuable tools and techniques. These resources not only assist in handling a setback's immediate aftermath but also clear the path to success and resilience over the long run.

- **Tools for Self-Assessment**: You can better understand how you respond to setbacks and pinpoint areas for growth by regularly evaluating yourself.
- **Objective-Setting Structures**: After a setback, defining specific, attainable goals can give you focus and inspiration.
- **Mechanisms of Feedback**: Receiving constructive criticism from mentors or peers is crucial for learning from failures.

Establishing a Helpful Environment to Overcome Obstacles

Having a supportive atmosphere around you is essential for overcoming difficulties. This comprises:
1. **Creating a Robust Support System**: It may be rather empowering to surround yourself with individuals who believe in your skills and abilities.
2. **Participating in Online Communities**: Joining forums or groups might offer more viewpoints and assistance.

Using Mindfulness to Help With Setback Coping

One effective strategy for reducing the tension and anxiety that frequently follow failures is mindfulness. Here are a few ideas for implementing mindfulness:
- **Conscious Breathing**: Mindful breathing is a valuable technique for stress relief and mental calmness.
- **Mindfulness Meditation**: Meditating regularly will help you deal with obstacles more composedly and skillfully.

Using Failures as Learning Opportunities

Recall that overcoming obstacles and failures is as significant as the final destination. Accept these situations as chances to develop, gain knowledge, and strengthen resilience.

Accepting Failure as a Necessity for Progress
If failure and setbacks are properly accepted, they can act as potent growth-promoting agents. They inspire us to think critically, be creative, and step outside our comfort zones. By changing the way we view failures, we can create new opportunities and successful routes.

Your Path Through Obstacles
As we draw to a close this extensive manual on handling failure and setbacks, keep in mind that every person's journey is different. Every obstacle you overcome presents a chance to become more innovative and robust. Using the skills and information you've acquired, keep going forward and use your failures as stepping stones to success.

Developing a Growth Mindset

A growth mindset can change how we face complex business problems and failures, increasing our success and pleasure.

There might be competition in the world. It takes more than simply more challenging work to stay ahead; you must also work smarter.

The growth mindset can help with that.

In most cases, it does not reflect their abilities or efforts when someone in a fast-paced, highly competitive sector isn't accomplishing their objectives or setting the correct priorities. It's usually the result of not having a growth attitude. You can progressively ascend to greater heights in your career with a growth mindset by only changing the way you think and live.

You're putting yourself in a position to learn a lot about the growth mindset by reading this article. We will assist you in defining it, nurturing it, and reaping its business and leadership rewards.

A Growth Mindset: What Is It?
The growth mindset is a way of thinking that supports the notion that intelligence and skill can

be acquired with patience, hard work, and devotion. With persistence and time, all of these elements of yourself are capable of development, evolution, and improvement. A growth mindset is an outlook that values resilience, learning from mistakes, and personal development.

Carol Dweck, a psychologist, initially presented this compelling viewpoint through her thorough studies on motivation, success, accomplishment, and mindset.

Dweck's research indicates that a "growth mindset" radically departs from the conventional "fixed mindset." People who have a fixed mindset think that their skills are fixed and unalterable. This may impede personal development and lead to self-imposed barriers.

People who have a growth mentality, on the other hand, welcome challenges, regard failure as a necessary step toward mastery, and think they have limitless potential. Setbacks do not discourage them; instead, they view them as stepping stones toward development and mastery. They know that talent and intelligence are malleable. It counts not only what you were born with, but also how much effort you're prepared to put in to grow and advance.

The value of a growth mindset is in its ability to enable you to become the best version of yourself, regardless of where you are in your journey.

Why Is It Important To Have A Growth Mindset?

It is essential to cultivate a growth mindset as it promotes resilience, eases learning, and drives achievement. It promotes the idea that obstacles are opportunities to grow in flexibility and problem-solving skills. Growth-minded people know that to succeed, they must push beyond their comfort zone, work hard, and learn from their mistakes.

A growth mentality can change how you handle obstacles and failures, increasing your success and contentment. It's not only about your thoughts; it's also about your actions and responses to the different circumstances life throws at you. You may perceive the opportunity for progress in every event if you have a mindset centered on learning and development.

The Advantages of a Growth Mindset

Enhanced resilience and motivation: People with a growth mindset are more likely to maintain their motivation despite obstacles. They are prepared to put in the required work to accomplish their goals because they recognize that patience and effort are essential components of success.

Adaptability to overcome obstacles: Growth-minded people know discomfort is the only way to experience personal development. They embrace challenging jobs with enthusiasm and the mindset of being "on the attack" rather than "on defense" instead of avoiding them.

Capacity to learn from mistakes and setbacks: People with a growth mindset can see mistakes and setbacks as opportunities for improvement. Knowing there will never be a straight path to improvement in anything significant makes it easier to learn from mistakes rather than give up.

Can One Develop a Growth Mindset?
Of course! A growth mindset is a perspective that may be developed and fostered over time rather than an innate one.

To cultivate a growth mentality, you must consciously change how you view obstacles, work, and criticism. Its main idea is that intelligence and aptitude are flexible qualities that can be refined through hard work and dedication. Furthermore, it's about believing in oneself and identifying possibilities for learning and improvement in every circumstance.

Recognizing the existence of a "fixed mindset" and learning how it shows up are the first steps toward developing a growth mindset. It could manifest as an aversion to difficulties, fear of failing, self-limiting beliefs, or a negative response to criticism. You can consciously change your attitude if you can identify these times.

For example, consider the following when faced with a challenging task: "What can I learn from this situation?"
"How can I grow from this?"

Examples of Growth Mindset
It is worthwhile to illustrate some of the two opposing viewpoints to understand better what a growth mindset entails. Here are a few helpful scenario examples: the

Situation	Fixed Mindset Methodology	Growth Mindset Methodology

You pass an exam with an extremely good grade.	Great! I must be really intelligent in this area	Fantastic! I had to put in a lot of effort and learn a lot.
You're starting a new assignment or project	I hope this will be easy for me	I hope this will be interesting!
You get negative feedback on your work	No way! This demonstrates my incompetence in this	Alright, I must return to my work and continue to learn.

These illustrations highlight the mentality differences. It's simple to blame innate talent for success or failure when taking a fixed mentality approach. You might turn to activities you know you're comfortable with to get comfort.

When you have a fixed perspective, you can acknowledge your efforts and endeavor to improve when you don't meet expectations. When you have the chance to learn something new, you can seek out challenges.

How To Gradually Adopt A Growth Mentality
You agree that having a growth mindset is a good concept. You are eager to take advantage of the chances it can present since you see its potential and revolutionary power.

But how can one genuinely develop a growth mindset?
Transitioning from a fixed to a progressive mentality is not as simple as turning on a light switch. The journey calls for thinking, practice, and deliberate effort. The good news, though? It's

doable, and we have nine tried-and-true methods to guide you.

1. Identify Traps in Fixed Mindsets

Understanding the fixed mindset, the opposite of the development mindset is the first step toward cultivating the latter. These are deep-rooted notions that your skills are fixed and unalterable. Have you ever encountered a weakness or shortcoming in yourself and said to yourself, "Well, that's just the way I am," or have you ever overcome a challenge and said, "That's just the way things are"? You can actively decide to take on a more adaptable mindset by marking these and seeing them as chances for development.

2. Accept Difficulties

Accepting problems in your life is a crucial step in your journey. When faced with obstacles, a person who has a growth mindset sees them as chances to improve and learn rather than as obstacles to be overcome. Modify your viewpoint. Consider every obstacle as a riddle to be solved, a mystery to be solved, or a contest to win. The idea is to change the mindset from "I can't do this" to "I can't do this yet." To improve, always remember that you must challenge yourself, get out of your comfort zone, and dare to do things you once believed were unachievable.

3. Have No Fear of Failure

What comes next? Rethink what failure means. Failure is not viewed as a dead end by those with a growth mindset. Instead, they see it as a teaching moment – a stepping stone toward achievement. Failure is a sign of bravery for daring to try, not inability. Don't let failure demoralize you the next time. Examine what went wrong, draw lessons from it, and apply what you've learned to improve the next time.

4. Consider Effort

Realize that the force behind progress is effort. Your work isn't in vain even when it feels like it's taking a while; it's helping you develop the grit and perseverance you'll need to reach your objectives. Establish clear, attainable goals that will take work to accomplish, and monitor your progress to make sure your efforts are going where they will have the most significant impact. It will be reaffirmed that skills may be developed and enhanced with time and effort if hard work and perseverance are valued and celebrated.

5. Keep Learning

A growth mindset's cornerstone is a strong desire to learn new things. It involves having a never-ending curiosity, looking for new information, and working tirelessly to improve. Make an effort to see every day as a chance to learn something new. Accept the thrill of learning, whether picking up a new skill for your job, exploring a subject you've always been curious about, or even learning a tasty new recipe.

6. **Develop Tenacity**

Growth mindsets are fueled by persistence. It's the determination to press on through difficult times. When faced with obstacles, people with a growth mentality consistently lean into the discomfort rather than pulling back into the safety of the familiar. It's second nature to them.

The key to perseverance with a development mindset is realizing that significant accomplishments take time and work. It's about valuing the process rather than just the result and enjoying the trip as much as the destination. It promotes a positive outlook on failure, seeing obstacles as helpful learning opportunities and essential components of personal development rather than as the end of the path.

7. **Look for Constructive Criticism**

Adopting a growth mindset requires the capacity to take constructive criticism and act upon it. It offers an external viewpoint that can draw attention to blind spots and development potential. Feedback is not a personal jab; instead, it's a tool for personal development.

Cultivating a growth mindset requires learning to seek out and be open to constructive criticism actively. Seek coworkers, coaches, or mentors who can offer you frank criticism. Use their feedback to hone your tactics, develop your abilities, and propel yourself.

8. **Be In The Company of Growth-Minded Individuals.**

Your company makes you who you are. Encountering others that share a growth mentality can significantly influence your path. You can be inspired and motivated by their optimistic outlooks, fortitude in adversity, and unwavering commitment to personal development. Additionally, they can offer priceless guidance, support, and inspiration while you forge your route toward development.

9. Enjoy Your Little Victories And Other People's Successes.

Accepting a development mentality is not seeing other people's success as a threat but as a source of inspiration. Honor your colleagues' successes and think about the lessons they have to teach you. You can grow with them by seeing how they achieved a goal, their tactics, and how they might be applied or modified to your circumstances. Finding inspiration in your environment is a beautiful and fulfilling experience.

Above all, remember to enjoy every tiny victory and accomplishment you achieve! Don't minimize yourself because you see people with more achievements than you. You can press on if you are grateful for your steady progress.

Accept The Power Of A Growth Mindset: The Adventure Begins Here

Adopting a growth mindset can have profound personal and professional transformations. A growth mindset gives you the willpower to overcome obstacles, the fortitude to pick yourself up after failing, and the drive to pursue your goals.

You can conquer the world like never before, thanks to the power of a development mentality.

- Recall that you are on a path toward growth.
- Obstacles present chances for development. Accept them.
- Failure does not mean loss. It's an educational opportunity.
- Mastery is reached via effort.
- Encourage a love of lifelong study.
- Seek out and value-helpful criticism.
- Put yourself in the company of growth-oriented people.

You're laying the groundwork for boundless career and personal development by implementing these techniques. Recall that developing and maintaining a growth mindset requires work. Although this path isn't always simple, it's one of the most fulfilling experiences. Now, take a deep breath, venture beyond your comfort zone, and immerse yourself in the growth mindset community. Your future self will be appreciative.

Seeking for Assistance and Resources

Seeking resources and help is a crucial but sometimes undervalued step in the complex process of developing resilience. Resilience isn't just about getting through terrible times on your own; it's also about realizing that human power can be significantly increased when we help one another out and apply every resource functional to us.

We must accept that we are not alone in navigating these choppy waters if we are to recover from life's disappointments fully. In this section, we'll explore the significance of seeking for resources and assistance for resilience, gaining knowledge from other viewpoints, and providing helpful guidance to help you strengthen your capacity to face hardship.

1. **The Influence of Social Networks:**

The importance of social support in fostering resilience has long been recognized. Our relationships with friends, family, and the community serve as safety nets, catching us when we fall. Consider a person who has lost a loved one; they often recover emotionally much more quickly when they are in the company of understanding friends and family. Support of this nature validates feelings on an emotional level, assisting people in grieving and strengthening their ability to bounce back from setbacks in life. It serves as a reminder that you are not facing difficulties alone.

2. **Professional Guidance and Therapy:**
Sometimes, the support of friends and family is insufficient to manage setbacks that are too overwhelming. Consulting a mental health expert can be very helpful. Psychologists, counselors, and therapists have the skills and information to guide clients through challenging emotional and psychological situations. This support can take many forms, such as helping you deal with anxiety, despair, or trauma, or it can just be a safe place for you to talk about your feelings. A therapist can assist you in creating coping mechanisms to face challenges and gradually increase your resilience.

3. **Developing Resilience with Self-Care:**
Although outside assistance is priceless, self-care is a vital component of resilience that shouldn't be disregarded. Exercise, meditation, and a healthy diet enhance physical and mental well-being and help you cope with life's obstacles. These self-care routines strengthen your inner fortitude and work as a proactive means of developing resilience. You become stronger and more resilient when you look after yourself.

4. **Education and Information:**
Since knowledge is a powerful tool, it can be an essential component of resilience. Knowledge about the science of resilience, coping mechanisms, and stress management can provide you with a toolset for overcoming adversity. Numerous books, online courses, and seminars offer insightful analysis and helpful guidance on developing resilience. Use these tools to improve your comprehension and capacity for recovery from setbacks.

5. **Communities and Support Groups:**
Joining communities of individuals who have gone through comparable struggles or support groups can be a tremendous source of strength. These groups allow people to exchange success stories, tactics, and experiences. These groups can be a safe sanctuary of empathy and shared knowledge, whether you're overcoming addiction, managing a chronic disease, or experiencing loss.

6. **Adaptive Problem-Solving:**
Being resilient involves more than just enduring hardship; it also entails creating original solutions to issues. You become more resilient by improving your problem-solving capacity and adjusting to

change. Resources like cognitive-behavioral therapy or problem-solving courses can give you the skills to overcome obstacles head-on.

7. **Positive Role Models:**
During trying times, mentors and role models may uplift and direct us. Having positive role models who have successfully navigated life's problems, be they a well-known individual who has overcome adversity or a personal mentor, can assist in molding your attitude to resilience. Their experiences and tales can provide insightful advice on how to overcome obstacles.

As you work to build resilience in your "Zone of Resistance," keep in mind that asking for help and assistance is a sign of strength and resolve to get over obstacles in life, not a sign of weakness. You may develop resilience and strengthen from life's challenges by combining social support, professional assistance, self-care, education, community, problem-solving techniques, and good role models.

Chapter 8

Embracing Change

Whether we like it or not, everything around us is ever-changing. The world constantly changes due to societal shifts and technological advancements, but it is crucial to remember that we continuously evolve. Despite this understanding, accepting change is one of the hardest lessons people must learn.

Change scares a lot of people. That is typical as well. Change is a constant reminder that we are becoming older, and there is something ominous and unsettling about this unavoidable aspect of aging.

Some view change and novelty as too complex, hazardous, and uncertain.
People would prefer to be unhappy than uncertain, as Tim Ferris famously observed, and science supports that. According to a recent neuroscience study, our brains register uncertainty like they

register errors. All we want is for it to be resolved so we can get comfortable again.

Accepting that things will not always go as planned is the first step towards embracing change. Though terrifying, this idea is also incredibly freeing. Accepting change is essential to your personal development and significantly impacts your level of happiness and success in general.

Let's explore this subject more and learn how to welcome change in your life.

Adapting to change

Working with people inevitably brings change, which is frequently a good thing. Adaptability to change can reduce stress and even boost output.

When you welcome and accept change, you can discover that new, exciting opportunities exist. While it may require patience and time to adjust to change, knowing how to deal with it will help you maintain your optimism.

It's possible that many of us have pondered, "How do you adapt to change? It's a challenging query.

The idea is to "adjust, adapt, and overcome," though, and this part will give you helpful advice to assist you in getting through any changes you may be facing with more ease.

Change: What is it?
Change occurs when an individual's or an organization's circumstances diverge from the preexisting norms and practices. This happens due to changing circumstances and experiences that demand new demands from people or organizations. For instance, you must adjust your daily routine, communications, and tasks to change jobs.

Adaptability: What is it?
The capacity to modify our attitudes, sentiments, and actions in response to novel, complicated, or complex circumstances is known as adaptability. It's a crucial quality that helps people deal with the ups and downs of life and react appropriately to unforeseen circumstances.

Key ideas on adaptability are as follows:
- It entails being adaptable and viewing change as a chance for personal development.

- Professionals, students, and those going through personal struggles can all benefit from having the ability to adapt.
- With effort and an attitude towards lifelong learning, it can be improved.

How does the ability to adapt function?

Being adaptable involves more than just weathering change—it also involves keeping a cheerful outlook. How, then, does it operate? In what ways does the psychology of change adaptation aid us in adjusting to novel circumstances?

The phases of adaptation include the following:

- **Consciousness**

This is when you realize something has changed or is about to change—being conscious aids in comprehending the change's nature and effects on you.

- **Acceptance**

Accepting the change is part of this. Acceptance means recognizing that a change is occurring and beginning to work with it rather than opposing it, not that you agree with the change.

- **Acquiring knowledge**

Learning or acquiring new skills is frequently necessary for adapting to change. This entails having an open mind, pursuing knowledge, and picking up knowledge from others.

- **Execution**

Here's where we apply everything we've learned. At this point, your adaptation efforts will be paying off, and you'll feel more confident handling comparable adjustments.

Advantages of Change Adaptation
We can develop, learn, and have more rewarding lives and careers if we adapt to change. The following are some advantages of change adaptation:

- **Lowering anxiety and tension**

Uncertainty brought on by change frequently results in worry. On the other hand, you can control these feelings if you can adjust to change. Accepting change helps us feel less stressed and anxious because it lessens our dread of the unknown.

- **Individual development**

We can acquire new knowledge, hone new talents, and better understand our capabilities when adjusting to change. We may promote personal development and strengthen our confidence and self-worth by pushing ourselves beyond our comfort zones and accepting change.

- **Improved output**

Performing well in a work environment or professional setting might result from adjusting to change. Those who adapt well are more likely to be the first to take advantage of the opportunities that change frequently provides, which can lead to career progress and greater job satisfaction.

- **Enhanced ability to solve problems**

Finding innovative answers to fresh problems is necessary for adjusting to change. As we become more adept at addressing and overcoming challenges, we may also lessen the stress and worry that comes with change by improving our problem-solving abilities.

- **An edge over competitors**

To stay ahead in the competitive world of today, adaptability is essential. Markets and industries are constantly changing, and those who can adjust rapidly stand to gain a great advantage. Those who are flexible as persons and as organizations can react to shifting trends and meet market demands efficiently, giving them a competitive advantage.

How to Adjust to Shift

There are many transitions in life, from minor to major and life-changing. This indicates that the capacity for change adaptation is an essential life skill rather than just a useful one.

The methods, exercises, and activities listed below will assist you in being more adaptable in your daily life.

Strategies for adjusting to change in the job and life

The development of adaptability is heavily dependent on techniques. Here are some scenarios to consider:

1. **Adopt a growth mindset:** Think of change as a chance for personal development and education. Consider obstacles transient and have faith in your capacity to adjust and triumph.
2. **Engage in self-reflection:** Give your values, objectives, and dreams some thought. Take advantage of this change to reflect and realign your path with your true self.

3. **Embrace adaptability**: Examine different viewpoints and question dogmatic mental processes. Embrace open-mindedness and curiosity to help you become more flexible in your thinking.
4. **Seek assistance:** Navigating change on your own may be very taxing. During trying circumstances, it is crucial to ask for help from friends, family, or professionals. Through communicating our worries and looking for direction, we can learn important lessons, receive support, and feel less alone.

Exercises for Adaptability

Exercise can support personal development and strengthen adaptive skills. The following activities will help you become more adaptable:

- **Journaling**: Discuss difficult circumstances you have encountered and the ways you overcame them. Consider the lessons you've learned and come up with some future-ready tactics.

- **Role-playing:** Get comfortable placing oneself in various situations that call for flexibility. To extend your thinking, investigate many viewpoints and consider alternate alternatives.

- **Meditation and mindfulness:** Practice mindfulness to develop nonjudgmental acceptance and present-moment awareness. This can assist you in reacting calmly and clearly to situations that change.
- **Volunteering**: Participate in community service initiatives or volunteer work to broaden your horizons and meet new challenges. This might expand your outlook and improve your flexibility.

- **Acquiring new abilities:** Look for chances to pick up new skills or delve into uncharted territories. Adaptability is fostered by accepting the learning process and pushing yourself beyond your comfort zone.

- **Accepting Change:** Look for chances to accept change voluntarily. This could be taking on new tasks at work or in your personal life, trying out new pastimes, or venturing into unfamiliar social situations.

Illustrations of adjusting to change

Here, we'll look at a few realistic cases to show how people can adjust to changes in their lives and careers.

A. Instances of adjusting to life's changes

Changing with the times might involve a range of situations that influence our development. These adjustments, whether foreseen or not, might affect our lives differently. Here are a few instances:

- **Change of career**

After years of employment in the same field, Amanda unexpectedly lost her job due to a company downsizing. Instead of experiencing failure, she saw this as a chance to explore a different professional direction.

Amanda took the time to evaluate her interests, abilities, and market needs. She changed her résumé to showcase transferable talents, networked with individuals in her target sector, and enrolled in pertinent courses. Amanda transitioned into a new career matching her hobbies because of her tenacity and adaptability.

- **Transfer**

Pios and Rolanda have spent their entire lives in a busy metropolis. However, they were forced to move to a tiny town due to financial difficulties. They were initially nervous about the move because they were leaving behind their social support system and familiar surroundings.

They interact with neighbors, join neighborhood clubs, and take part in community events as a way to adjust to this life transition. Pios and Rolanda find new chances, forge meaningful connections, and establish a sense of belonging in their new home by being open and willing to embrace the new surroundings.

- **Adjusting a relationship**

After a protracted courtship, Festus and Bella marry and move in together. They encounter difficulties making concessions and modifying one another's inclinations and habits as their lives and routines collide. They actively listen to each other's needs, communicate openly and honestly, and devise innovative ways to keep their relationship supportive and harmonious. At the same time, they adjust to this shift in their lives.

B. **Examples of how the workplace has changed**

Because of changing business plans, new positions, and team changes, workplace dynamics are constantly changing. Here are a few such instances of adjusting to changes inside an organization:

- **Accepting new technology**

Project manager Terry noticed a shift in work ethics after introducing new project management software. Alex decided to seize the chance for career advancement rather than fight the change. He actively looked for training materials, went to webinars, and worked with coworkers familiar with the program.

- **Making the switch to remote work**

Due to a worldwide pandemic, Diana, a marketing specialist, had to adjust to a significant shift when her employer moved to remote work. Rather than giving in to overwhelming feelings, she swiftly changed her work environment at home, established a schedule, and investigated several digital collaboration platforms to guarantee smooth communication with her colleagues.

- **Getting Used to Reorganisation in Organisations**

Within her company, Priscilla, a top executive, had to deal with a significant organizational upheaval.

Instead of experiencing resistance or demotivation, she embraced the transition as a chance to reinterpret her job and further the company's expansion. Karen asked for and received feedback from her superiors, actively sought opportunities to provide value, and modified her abilities to fit the changing demands of the company.

Frequently held beliefs about adjusting to change

The ability to adjust to change is increasingly crucial in our fast-paced society. However, a few myths frequently prevent people from successfully embracing change.

Let's examine a few common misconceptions and dispel them.

1. **Getting used to change implies being weak or giving up.**

In actuality, adapting to change is a strength rather than a sign of weakness or failure. It entails moving beyond one's comfort zone and seizing fresh chances for advancement and self-improvement.

2. **Giving in to change implies sacrificing one's morals and principles.**

It's not always necessary to compromise your morals and ideas to adjust to change. It involves adopting an adaptable mindset and figuring out how to deal with novel events while adhering to your fundamental values.

3. To adapt to change is to go past the past.

Getting over the past is not the same as adjusting to change. Whether good or bad, our past experiences have shaped who we are now. They offer insightful knowledge, practical skills, and significant transferable lessons to other contexts. To adjust to change, we must incorporate what we have learned from the past into the present.

4. Change adaptation is never easy and can be rather stressful.

Change does not always have to be unpleasant and stressful, even though it can sometimes be. Developing resilience and mastering applicable coping mechanisms to control tension and discomfort is essential to adapting to change.

5. Only during significant life events is it vital to adapt to change.

It's essential to learn how to adjust to change in all facets of life, not just significant life events. Routines, relationships, the workplace, and personal objectives all change. People who can embrace change and adjust to new situations are better able to take advantage of opportunities, stay relevant, and live happy, fulfilled lives.

Overcoming Obstacles to Shift Adaptation

Accepting change is not always straightforward, and some people may run into several obstacles along the path. Here are a few challenges with adjusting to change and workable ways to get past them.

Fear of what's not known

Our capacity to adjust to change can be hampered by fear and uncertainty when confronted with the unknown. One or more of the following actions are necessary to overcome this obstacle:

- **Embrace your fears:** Understand that fear is a common reaction to change.
- **Focus on the possibilities:** Change your perspective to consider the advantages that change may present rather than dwelling on the drawbacks of the uncertainty.
- **Make tiny steps:** Divide the transformation into doable goals or actions. You may progressively increase your confidence and lessen your fear of the unknown by making baby movements ahead.

Opposition to Change

A common obstacle in life and professional transitions is resistance to change. Here's how to get around this:

- **Seek assistance:** Create a network of mentors, family members, and friends who can support and mentor you during this transition journey. Their viewpoints and experiences can assist you in breaking through resistance and gaining fresh perspectives.
- **Reframe change as a decision:** Acknowledge that while change is unavoidable, choosing to welcome it is a deliberate decision. You can reclaim control and empowerment by redefining change as an active choice instead of something imposed upon you.

Insufficient Adaptability

Inflexible expectations and prior assumptions can hamper our capacity to navigate novel situations successfully. Here are several strategies to get beyond this obstacle:

- Examine your expectations, presumptions, and beliefs by engaging in self-reflection. In the face of change, are they doing an

excellent job for you? Be willing to question and modify your viewpoints to better fit the changing circumstances.
- Develop emotional fortitude and coping mechanisms to strengthen your resilience. People who possess resilience can overcome obstacles and adjust to changes with more ease.
- Adopt a growth-oriented mindset by viewing change as an opportunity to learn and improve. Consider every new encounter a chance to learn something new and acquire new abilities.

Getting Over the Past

Traumas and past experiences can significantly influence our capacity to welcome change and grasp new chances. The following techniques will assist you in overcoming this obstacle:
- **Seek professional assistance:** You might want to think about consulting with a therapist or counselor if your past experiences have a significant influence on your capacity to adjust. They can offer you support and aid in the processing of unprocessed feelings.
- **Develop self-compassion** by treating yourself with kindness and gentleness while

you adjust to change. Recognize that carrying emotional baggage is common, and allow yourself to heal and develop at your speed.
- **Concentrate on the here and now:** Pay attention to the current opportunities rather than ruminating on the past. Use grounding exercises and mindfulness to help you maintain your attention in the present moment.

Converting Obstacles Into Chances

There are obstacles in life at all times. The way that successful people tackle these obstacles sets them apart from others who struggle. Successful people view obstacles as opportunities for development and advancement.

When faced with obstacles, it's simple to feel overwhelmed and want to give up. Nonetheless, obstacles can be transformed into chances for development and achievement if one has the appropriate perspective. Our capacity to regulate our attitudes and thoughts about what we meet gives the mindset power.

Here, I will discuss strategies for transforming setbacks into chances for achievement. It's critical to realize that every obstacle may present a secret opportunity. We can use our challenges as stepping stones to accomplish our goals if we adopt this approach.

Never forget that every obstacle we face is a hidden opportunity. This kind of thinking is essential to success and overcoming setbacks. By taking this method, we may overcome obstacles and achieve success more efficiently.

Here are some tips for converting obstacles into opportunities:

1. **Accepting Change**

Accepting change is essential in the fast-paced world of today. See change as an opportunity to learn and grow rather than something to be afraid of. Though it may feel overwhelming at first, change may lead to growth and create doors to new opportunities. Experiencing things beyond your comfort zone can lead to some of the most memorable moments.

Think back to the times in the past when you handled change well and achieved your goals.

These accomplishments show that you can adapt to change and even thrive in it. Promote an environment where people on your team or in your company are open to change and are always looking for ways to do things better. This adaptable and creative strategy may result in long-term success.

Although it can be difficult, adapting to change is necessary to stay competitive and grow. If you approach change with optimism, you'll find that it frequently promotes ingenuity and flexibility and leads to both professional and personal progress.

2. Positivity of Thought

Making the most of opportunities and overcoming obstacles requires a positive outlook. It entails focussing on solving issues rather than wallowing in them. You lay a solid foundation for your success and personal development when you embrace this mindset.

It's critical to recognize that unexpected solutions can arise from having an optimistic mindset. Having an optimistic outlook on challenges makes you more innovative and resourceful in your problem-solving. In addition, you foster a pleasant, upbeat atmosphere where everyone can prosper together by encouraging those around you to do the same.

To summarise, the secret to transforming obstacles into opportunities is to develop an optimistic outlook. Solutions-oriented thinking and encouraging positivism in yourself and others create the conditions for individual development and a more encouraging community.

3. Acquiring Knowledge from Setbacks

Seeing setbacks as teaching moments is essential for developing oneself. When you have a setback, reflect on what went wrong and how you might improve for the future. Recall that failure is a necessary step on the path to success; it is not the total reverse of success.

Establishing an atmosphere where making errors is accepted as a necessary learning component is crucial to adopting this way of thinking. It's important to stress that it's acceptable to make mistakes along the path and to support others in being honest about their mistakes. You'll create a culture in which people recognize that failure can yield important lessons and, eventually, tremendous success if you use this approach.

Therefore, remember that failure is a bump leading to achievement. Keep going forward, make improvements, and remember that every setback is a step closer to your destination.

4. Scheduling

Strategic planning is an essential instrument that enables you to foresee and prepare for possible challenges. By carefully considering potential difficulties, you can design practical solutions.

It's crucial to keep your plan in mind after you've created it. Instead, set aside time to examine and revise your tactics regularly. Your plans must change as the world does since it is continually changing.

Challenges are not something to be afraid of; instead, see them as a chance to improve your plans. Take advantage of the opportunity to review and improve your strategies when challenged. Engage your team in strategic conversations to arrive at the best decisions. Various viewpoints can inspire more creative and reliable solutions.

5. Requesting Input

Receiving feedback is crucial for both your career and personal development. Seeking input from mentors, customers, and friends can help you become a better professional. Rather than being terrified of criticism, embrace it as an opportunity to improve. Encouraging others to provide feedback and demonstrating your regard for their opinions can significantly influence.

Feedback is like gold when it comes to personal and professional development. Make it a practice to discover what your friends, mentors, and clients think of your work. Accept criticism to help you improve and reach your full potential. Establish an atmosphere where individuals are at ease offering their thoughts and know you value them.

Recall that constructive criticism is your best tool for improving yourself. Engage with peers, mentors, and clients frequently and listen to their opinions. Although receiving criticism can be difficult, you must improve. If you create an environment where people are comfortable sharing their ideas, you will advance tremendously.

6. Making the Most of Resources

Resources can be used effectively to turn obstacles into opportunities. Realizing the full range of resources at your disposal—including people, technology, and information—is crucial. When faced with obstacles, use your imagination to determine how to make the most of these resources. Encourage ingenuity among your team members as well to realize their full potential.

You may realize your potential for success and advancement by using the already accessible resources. Begin by determining who possesses the knowledge and abilities required to address particular difficulties. Make use of technology to obtain essential data and expedite procedures. Encourage your coworkers to be resourceful by fostering an environment that rewards creativity and pushing them to think beyond conventional answers to challenges.

Ultimately, being resourceful is essential to conquering challenges and realizing your objectives. It's about utilizing your resources as efficiently as possible, whether human capital, tools, or expertise. Through the facilitation of resourcefulness among team members and the utilization of abundant resources, obstacles can be effectively overcome and converted into chances for advancement.

7. Collaboration and Networking

Collaboration and networking are effective strategies that can lead to discovering new prospects. An excellent place to start is establishing relationships with individuals and businesses in your sector. Collaborating on projects with others might provide you with new insights and inspiration. Also, in trying times, your network may be an excellent resource for support and guidance.

Never undervalue the significance of building relationships. These relationships may open up unique opportunities that you would not otherwise discover. You can increase your knowledge and view things from various perspectives when you work as a team. And having a solid support system can be invaluable when times are tough.

Thus, keep in mind to grow your network and be receptive to working together. It's an excellent opportunity to open doors to new prospects, acquire insightful knowledge, and have a solid support network for your career.

8. Ongoing Education

Ongoing education is necessary to address obstacles adequately. It entails remaining current with the newest techniques and trends in the field. You can remain competitive in your field and adjust to new conditions by doing this.

Creating an environment where learning is valued within your company is another essential component of continuous learning. Urge your coworkers to accept lifelong learning as an integral aspect of their jobs. As a result, your team may become more innovative and adept at addressing problems.

Finally, I see every obstacle as an opportunity to develop. Consider challenges as chances to learn new perspectives and abilities rather than as barriers. By tackling obstacles with an open mind, you may strengthen your resilience and improve your ability to deal with whatever comes your way.

9. Adaptability and Flexibility

Being flexible and adaptable is essential in today's ever-changing world. To succeed, you must be able to modify your tactics in response to emerging difficulties quickly. This entails having an open mind and being adaptable to change on both a personal and team level.

It's critical to promote an open-minded mindset among your team. Your organization's collective intelligence can be tapped into by creating an atmosphere that values and embraces fresh ideas. This receptivity to different viewpoints makes it possible to solve problems creatively and opens the door to novel ideas.

Ultimately, the ability to bounce back from setbacks is crucial. There will always be ups and downs, but knowing when to give up might be the difference between success and failure. We frequently learn and develop the most from these difficulties, eventually making us more capable of navigating the constantly shifting terrain of our world.

10. Contemplative Methodology

Frequent introspection is an effective strategy that improves your ability to handle difficulties. Setting aside time for introspection on a personal and professional level is crucial. Finding your strengths and shortcomings via reflection can be quite beneficial. Encourage your team or organization to develop the practice of introspection rather than keeping it to yourself.

Regularly pausing to reflect can significantly impact how you tackle life's challenges. Don't forget to schedule time for introspection in your personal and professional lives. Using introspection, you can acquire a profound understanding of your strengths and areas for development. Promote reflection among your team or organization; it's not only a personal exercise.

It's a wise decision to include introspection in your daily activities. It gives you a better sense of your talents, enabling you to tackle obstacles head-on. Recall that cultivating a culture of reflection throughout your group can lead to more significant growth and success, just as important as improving yourself.

In summary

It's a solid ability to turn obstacles into possibilities. It calls for a unique style of thinking. This way of thinking not only makes things more accessible for people to get through difficult situations, but it also makes them stronger.

Using this strategy involves shifting our perspective on issues. We might see them as opportunities to grow rather than obstacles to overcome. This shift in viewpoint may result in more beneficial fixes and advancements.

We do more than overcome difficult times when we turn obstacles into possibilities. They make us stronger and more capable than we were before. Growth and development are essential processes for both people and organizations.

Flexibility and Agility in Decision Making

In the dynamic and unpredictable world of today, team leaders must make choices that support adaptability and agility. While flexibility refers to the openness to consider many ideas and viewpoints, agility refers to the capacity to respond swiftly and efficiently to changing circumstances. How can you make choices that allow your team to be flexible and agile? Here are a few tactics to think about.

1. **Establish mutually understood and explicit goals.**

The goals' degree of clarity and alignment is one of the significant variables influencing decision-making. Your team can make decisions that support the shared vision and prevent confusion or conflicts if they clearly understand what they want to accomplish. Setting and sharing clear goals requires regular communication, feedback, and goal-adjustment as necessary. Additionally, you must make sure that your team members comprehend how their choices fit with the organization's principles and values and how they advance the overall objectives.

2. **Include your teammates.**

Including your team members in the decision-making process is another method for reaching judgments that encourage adaptability and agility. You can use their varied perspectives, expertise, and skill sets by asking for their thoughts, ideas, and suggestions. Additionally, you can raise their ownership of the decisions and level of engagement and dedication. You need to foster an environment of cooperation, transparency, and trust if you want your team members to be involved. Practical techniques for consensus-building, brainstorming, and providing feedback must also be used.

3. **Try things out and pick up tips.**

To make judgments that foster flexibility and agility, a third tactic is to try new things and learn from your mistakes. Rather than following a single strategy or plan, you might experiment, assess, and compare the outcomes. You can find fresh possibilities, grow from your failures, and perform better by doing this. It is essential to have a development mentality, promote creativity, and applaud mistakes if you want to experiment and learn.

In addition, you must measure your progress, gather and evaluate data, and make any necessary corrections.

4. Assign and confer authority

A fourth tactic for decision-making that fosters adaptability and agility is to assign tasks and give team members more authority. You may empower people to make appropriate decisions for their circumstances and environment by granting them greater freedom and accountability. Additionally, you can quicken things, boost motivation, and lessen bottlenecks.

To empower and delegate, you must set clear expectations, give direction, and show support to your team members. In addition, you must keep an eye on outcomes, offer criticism, and acknowledge accomplishments.

5. **Examine and consider**

Evaluating and considering your decision-making procedure and results is the sixth tactic for reaching conclusions that foster adaptability and agility. You'll be able to determine what succeeded, what failed, and what needs improvement by doing this. In addition, you can impart best practices, apply lessons discovered, and draw insights from your experience. You must plan regular meetings, pose questions, and actively listen to assess and reflect. Additionally, you must convey and record your decisions, actions, and outcomes.

The Significance of Swiftness in Making Decisions

1. **Quicker reaction to shifts in the market:**

Being nimble in one's decision-making process allows one to react swiftly to changes in the market. Market conditions can change quickly in today's dynamic economic world. Thus, companies must be prepared to adjust their strategy quickly. Businesses may take advantage of new possibilities, keep ahead of developing trends, and reduce risks by using agility in their decision-making processes. To meet client requests and achieve a competitive edge, a retail company might promptly modify its inventory and marketing methods in response to a sudden rise in demand for a particular product.

2. **Increased originality and inventiveness:**
Making decisions quickly also encourages an innovative and creative culture in businesses. Workers are more likely to feel empowered to think creatively and unconventionally and to suggest novel solutions when adaptable decision-making procedures are receptive to fresh perspectives. This may result in innovative concepts, better goods or services, and, eventually, a more potent competitive advantage. Companies such as Google and Apple, for example, are renowned for making decisions quickly, a quality that has enabled them to innovate and upend their respective industries consistently.

3. **Higher levels of client satisfaction:**
Organizations can better satisfy the requirements and expectations of their customers by making decisions with agility. The consumer wants, and tastes can shift quickly, and companies that adjust their strategy fast enough to meet these changes have a higher chance of success.

For instance, the world's largest online retailer, Amazon, is well known for its customer-centric business model. It continuously evaluates user input and data to make snap judgments about what products to offer, how to deliver them, and how much to charge. Amazon's reputation for providing exceptional customer service and having high customer satisfaction levels can be attributed to its adaptability.

Chapter 9

Staying Motivated

When things get hard, motivation keeps you going toward your objectives, gets you out of bed in the morning, and keeps you focused on completing a task.

Motivation: What is it?
Motivation is the desire to fulfill your needs or reach your goals.

It is impacted by the following factors:
- how much you want the goal
- what you stand to gain
- what you stand to lose by not reaching the objective.
- Your standards

The desire to alter something in one's life is universal. But finding the willpower even to begin might be difficult. To discover your methods of becoming motivated, it is helpful to understand what motivation means to you.

However, motivation can be in both good and bad ways:
- Positive reinforcement centers on the benefits that will result from taking action. For instance: "Completing this assignment will put me one step closer to being qualified."
- The negative consequences of inaction are the main emphasis of negative incentives. In this situation, "I will jeopardize my studies if I do not finish this task within a few hours."

In certain situations, both positive and negative incentives can be successful. Nevertheless, acting on your desire is far simpler than doing so to prevent a particular result if you don't act. Negative motivation might make you feel helpless and even lower your motivation if you don't have a constructive action plan.

Why does motivation matter?
Motivation is crucial because it:
- Gives you objectives to strive for and
- Facilitates problem-solving.
- Aids in breaking old behaviors
- Overcoming opportunities and difficulties

How can I become motivated?

Motivation is a problem for most people, but it can be challenging if you suffer from mental health conditions like anxiety or depression. Here are some pointers:

- Decide on one clear, attainable goal for yourself.
- Consider how to incorporate that objective into your life and what steps to take to get there. Next, set a deadline (like a week or a month, whatever works).
- Divide your objective into manageable, minor activities and schedule regular reminders to finish each.
- Tell your loved ones about your objectives and ask them to help you stay motivated. Use your network of friends and family as support.

How to handle losing motivation

Although setbacks are inevitable, you can pick up where you left off by strengthening your resilience.

The following advice will assist you in rediscovering your motivation:

- Check your goals to be sure they can be accomplished in the time frame you have given. You could need to divide your objective into more manageable, smaller goals.
- Recall your initial motivation or reason for wanting to accomplish that goal.
- Look to people for inspiration and allow literature to impact you. Consult with your mentor and family members or friends who have achieved similar goals to yours.
- There are moments when you must stop and begin again.

Where to Look for Assistance
- Speak to a trusted friend or a counselor if you are having trouble staying motivated; they can offer helpful coping mechanisms.
- A mental health care plan may cover counseling expenses if you qualify for one and have a mental illness. Confer your doctor for direction on this.

Identifying Intrinsic Motivation

From an early age, we are frequently trained to look for outside incentives or avoid penalties, such as receiving a sticker for finishing homework or being grounded for disobeying an order. Although these techniques might seem helpful in the short run, they do not inspire long-term motivation. For instance, a lot of kids struggle to maintain their motivation to do chores in the absence of an external incentive. Intrinsic motivation is relevant in this situation.

Extrinsic motivation (sometimes referred to as external motivation) and intrinsic motivation (often referred to as internal motivation) are the two categories of motivation.

We can access a more rewarding and long-lasting source of motivation by concentrating on internal variables like enjoyment, personal curiosity, or a desire for personal improvement.

We will explore intrinsic motivation in more detail and guide you in identifying and using your internal motivation in this section.

Intrinsic motivation: what is it?
It is the motivation or desire to do something for its own sake without regard to pressures or benefits from outside sources. It comes from within and is driven by a person's interests,

pleasure, or sense of accomplishment from the task at hand.

Intrinsically motivated individuals are propelled by internal forces, such as a desire for knowledge acquisition, exploration, creation, mastery, or personal development. Because they are driven by internal needs rather than by pressures or rewards from outside sources, they derive greater pleasure and fulfillment from their work or activities. Better performance, inventiveness, and tenacity result from this, as does psychological health.

Developing a hobby, picking up a new skill or language for personal growth, or engaging in an activity or sport just for fun are all behaviors driven by internal motivation.

Why Self-Induced Motivation Is Superior to External Motivation

In general, we're all in need of inspiration. Extrinsic rewards are not nearly as effective as internal incentives in creating a persistent motivation to "do something," according to extensive studies in the field.

No

Why? It's easy. There is a significant difference between acting out of "you must" and acting out of "you want to."

Consider the most evident example that exists: labor.

How much joy will your employment bring you if you arrive at work each day fearing the day that lies ahead? What about outcomes and productivity? Work quality?

Yes, you are correct; you won't be at the top of the list for Employee of the Month very soon. The short-lived nature of external incentives is a problem.
How long does the "high" you receive when you get promoted after completing 100-hour work weeks last?

According to research, the sensation of being on cloud ninety minutes lasts just briefly and leaves you wanting more. As a result, you are trapped in an endless cycle known as the "hedonic treadmill," when you can only be inspired by more substantial and dazzling things, only to discover that when you acquire them, they don't fulfill your expectations. Alternatively, as brilliantly stated by writer and journalist Oliver Burkeman: "Write every day" won't work unless you enjoy writing. Furthermore, no fitness program will endure if you don't find any degree of enjoyment in the activity.

The Advantages of Intrinsic Motivation

Long-term job performance is better predicted by intrinsic motivation than by extrinsic incentive. One explanation is that when we have an internal motivation, we behave just out of enjoyment for the task. We continue daily because we are motivated, inspired, content with who we are, and joyful.

A further explanation is that internally motivated attitudes are linked to concepts like having a greater purpose, supporting a cause, or acting in a way that benefits or transcends ourselves. According to research, using praise or other external motivators to boost students' motivation from within ultimately leads to "slower acquisition of skills and more errors in the learning process."

On the other hand, internally motivated youngsters actively seek out difficulties and show more significant involvement in the work at hand.

Thus, it appears that all of the study points towards one crucial finding: intrinsic drive is essential to avoid the boredom that arises from thinking about what needs to be done or what you should accomplish.

How to Unlock Your innate Motivation

Suppose you have to excavate a ditch. If they weren't compensated or coerced into doing it, many people could view this as a task they would neither want nor love. As you have been following along, they are both examples of extrinsic motivators. But what if you were excavating the ditch to build a swimming pool that would bring years of fun to you and your loved ones? For most people, including you, this would undoubtedly change things.

Though these may seem like irrelevant ideas, they are a type of "growth motivation," as defined by psychologist Abraham Maslow: the drive to go beyond merely meeting one's basic requirements.

All of us have a hierarchy of needs, according to Maslow. He postulated that an individual's pursuit of five fundamental needs—physiological, safety, social, esteem, and self-actualization—leads to motivation. He postulated further that these demands can result in psychological stresses that affect how someone behaves. Our drive for self-fulfilment and self-actualization are components of growth motivation.

So tell me, how does your inner motivation relate to all of this "psychobabble"?

Your innate motivation can be unlocked by utilizing the psychobabble. You can redirect your attention from any external reward to this place once you know where your internal growth originates. When you do this, you'll discover that labor turns into enjoyment and suffering into advancement, contributing to your personal development.

You will have years of success and enjoyment there, just like it has for me. It is a genuinely fantastic location. But, you might wonder, how?

The following five short suggestions can help you boost your intrinsic motivation:

1. Examine every aspect of the task or scenario you are faced with initially.
2. Dissect it into its parts: what, how, and why?

3. Pay attention to the element that will make you feel good about yourself.
4. Make this the main focus of the exercise.
5. Consider and express thankfulness for this aspect, if not for everything.

Six(6) Strategies to Boost Your innate drive

So, how can one obtain more of the good stuff, or more specifically, how can one develop internal motivation?

You can do a lot of actions to increase your drive. These are the most highly ranked.

1. Self-Sufficiency

In 1982, Albert Bandura, an American-Canadian psychologist, created the self-efficacy theory. Efficacy is our conviction that we can accomplish the objectives we set for ourselves.

Put otherwise, the question is whether we believe we have "what it takes" to succeed in our chosen field. The relationship between self-efficacy and improved motivation, better performance, and increased self-esteem is easily seen. Individuals with a strong sense of their abilities are inclined to strive more, set more challenging objectives, and be more motivated to improve their work.

As a result, having confidence in our ability to succeed acts as a self-fulfilling prophecy, inspiring us to work even harder to convince ourselves that we can.

2. Connect Your Deeds to a Higher Goal

Discovering your life's purpose is crucial. This implies that you must be very clear about your motivations and the reasons behind your actions.
For you, what brings you intrinsic satisfaction? This is known as "reframing your narrative" by psychologists.

It's inspiring. Rephrasing how you do can benefit others and make a difference in the universe can be a strong motivator and source of purpose.

3. Offer Assistance

An excellent method to give back to the world is by volunteering. Helping you feel significant in helping the less fortunate, gaining new skills, feeling good about yourself, or connecting to some of your inner values, like kindness and humanitarianism, can also increase your internal motivation.

When you put aside all expectations for external rewards and act out of sheer joy and fulfillment from bettering the lives of others, you are acting from intrinsic motivation.

4. Act Now Rather Than Waiting to "Feel Like It"

As an excellent article in the Harvard Business Review clarifies, what we mean when we say things like "I can't make myself go to the gym" or "I can't get up early" is that we don't feel like it. Other than being lazy, nothing psychologically keeps us from completing such tasks.

The truth is, though, that you don't need to "feel like it" to act.

It happens sometimes that even though you may not want to do anything at first, once you get going, you find your intrinsic desire and become motivated.

For example, after a long day at work, you don't feel like going to the gym, so you don't spend hours "for and against" it in your mind. Remind yourself that you'll consider it later. You will feel less worn out and uninspired as soon as you enter the gym and are surrounded by like-minded people.

Setting up and adhering to routines is another strategy for overcoming procrastination. It won't be as horrible to get up at six a.m. for work or to write for an hour every day once the habit takes hold.

5. Independence

The self-motivation theory was developed by two psychology professors at the University of Rochester in the middle of the 1980s: Richard Ryan and Edward Deci.

One of the most well-known theories in motivation studies it emphasizes the various intrinsic and extrinsic motivators that influence human behavior. The idea goes on to say that we can satisfy our desire for growth by focusing on three basic needs: relatedness, autonomy, and competence.

We will be more motivated to give it our all and perform better if our employment provides us with opportunities to learn and develop and the freedom to think creatively and accomplish things on our own terms. Furthermore, because we are social creatures, people require a sense of belonging and respect from others.

Even when we feel uninspired and unmotivated, these sources of intrinsic drive, both alone and in combination, can act as potent catalysts to keep us thriving.

6. Reach a Higher Motivation

An intriguing study conducted in 2016 tried to understand how motivated high-achieving workers stay when their employer cannot provide them with internal or external motivation. The study followed employees in a Mexican plant who performed the same routine jobs every day with almost little opportunity for professional growth, skill acquisition, or promotion. All were paid the same, no matter how well they performed. Thus, the only extrinsic incentive was to maintain one's employment.

Last Words

When enhancing our general well-being and discovering lasting enjoyment and fulfillment in all we do, intrinsic motivation is the deciding factor.

The next time you struggle to complete a task, try associating it with a goal more significant than yourself, ideally with intangible rewards.

Acknowledging Advancement And Commemorating Successes

Accomplishment should be rewarded when an organization is transforming. Acknowledging achievements and rewarding success not only inspires and motivates workers but also serves to reinforce the improvements and advancements accomplished. Acknowledging advancement and commemorating successes encourage staff members to keep working towards the organization's objectives by serving as a reminder of the value of change.

Here are some pointers:

1. Recognise Little Wins:
- Celebrate every success, no matter how tiny. Reward yourself when you finish a difficult chapter, ace a practice exam, or reach a study objective.
- Example: Let's say you've been unable to understand a complex subject for a while, and now you do. Reward yourself with a pat on the back for your accomplishments.

2. Establish Milestone Awards:
- Divide your academic path into discrete stages. Prepare a reward for every goal attained.

- For instance, reward yourself with a favorite dinner, a movie night, or a soothing spa treatment after a week of regular study sessions.

3. Establish a menu for rewards:
- Create a list of incentives that speak to you. These can range in size from minor to major.
- Bronze Level (Daily): Suck back a cup of your preferred joe.
- Silver Level (Weekly): Feel free to binge-watch an episode of your preferred television program.
- Monthly Gold Level: Invest in that book you've had your eye on.

4. Social Celebrations:
- Tell your loved ones, study partners, and friends about your accomplishments. Their support can increase your drive.
- As an illustration, throw a virtual celebration with pals when you reach a significant exam benchmark. Join in on games, conversations, and celebrations.

5. Mindful Self-Care:

- There are other ways to reward yourself besides material goods. Make self-care activities a priority, such as walking, exercising, or meditation.
- For instance, take a quick stroll outdoors or engage in deep breathing exercises to relax after a demanding study session.

6. See the Reward:
- Envision the happiness you will feel after reaching your objectives and getting the rewards. Motivation can be increased through visualization.
- Consider yourself having a well-earned day off or celebrating with friends.

7. Steer clear of guilt:
- Some business owners feel bad about rewarding themselves or taking pauses. Recall that productivity depends on taking care of oneself.
- For instance, acknowledge that viewing a movie requires mental refreshment rather than feeling bad about it.

Recall that acknowledging accomplishments is essential for preserving mental health when preparing for exams; it is not frivolous. By using these techniques, you'll maintain your motivation and focus and manage stress well.

Part 5

Sustainability and Long-Term Success

"Sustainability is not just a trend; it's a strategic imperative. Those who embrace it will thrive in the long run."

Tim Cook, CEO of Apple Inc.

Chapter 10

Sustainable Habits

The topic of sustainability is gaining global attention. While some are debating and conversing, others are acting. While some do less, some do more. Acting is the most crucial thing to accomplish. You. Me. Everyone. for the future.

Sustainable Habits: What Are They?
Sustainable habits are ones that both improve our quality of life and safeguard the environment.

Developing Routines and Rituals

The success of a person who effectively organizes their life is probably greatly influenced by their routines and rituals. Here are some reasons why creating routines and rituals may be beneficial, regardless of your goals—maintaining sobriety, adopting suitable coping mechanisms for a mood or behavioral condition, or realizing that more excellent structure is necessary for your power as an individual.

What Separates Rituals from Routines?

A routine can be defined as "a sequence of actions regularly followed; a fixed program" or simply as your go-to method of accomplishing things. Maybe you have your coffee maker programmed to start at the same time every morning by setting it up the night before. Your dog may follow the same route every day on their first stroll. The following are some advantages of creating routines:

Following a sleep hygiene regimen, which includes turning off electronics an hour before bed, meditating, reading gently, and taking care of yourself, keeps you healthy and improves your sleep quality the following day.

- As you establish a routine that helps you stay focused, you'll "waste less physical energy and brain space."
- More time spent with the people and things you wish to do that you enjoy
- "Reduce the number of decisions you have to make each day for a deeper sense of peace as well as relaxation of the mind and body" is one benefit of routine repetition.

Although rituals are often connected to religious or spiritual ceremonies, they may also be defined as "an act or sequence of acts regularly repeated in a set, precise manner," which sounds much like a routine. The distinction lies in purpose: whereas many routines are helpful with a specific objective in mind, a routine can be elevated to the status of a ritual with a clear intention. This is why rituals are necessary for several reasons, such as:

- To help us stay connected to what really matters and keep our priorities in check.
- Please assist us in remaining rooted not only in life but also in our fundamental principles and the reasons behind them.
- As a kind of ritual that is required every day, whether it be spiritual or not, to "boost physical and mental well-being."

Chopra says that rituals can boost our confidence, make us feel more secure, lighten the load of grief, and help ease anxiety in our busy lives. Above all, rituals are a guaranteed way to make people happier.

Regulars to Support Your Lifestyle
We comprehend the interdependent levels among circumstances like:

- Problems related to substance usage
- Grief, PTSD, and trauma
- Co-occurring illnesses
- eating disorders
- Drug withdrawal
- Process abnormalities
- Mood disorders

After receiving necessary medical care, a patient's continuum of care plan may include other holistic, whole-food-based health management strategies, regular exercise, 12-step program support, and other alternatives. Routine structure gives you equilibrium in your daily performance and emotional state, laying the groundwork for success in these and other aspects of your life.

Advice for Creating Routines

I've included some advice on creating essential self-care habits that are effective for you:

- Make a list of everything you need to accomplish every day to start. This might be as simple as cleaning your teeth or having a shower, or it could be more involved, like getting your kids ready for school, working out, and making nutritious meals.

- Next, consider the hours of the day or night when you are most focused and energized. This is the time to plan out particular activities and routines.
- Using this knowledge, create routines that support your goals, enhance your well-being, and help you streamline essential chores.
- Start your day with the most exciting things and connect you to your mission or passion. By taking this step, you can increase your regular accountability and make sure you finish the tasks that are most crucial to your well-being.
- Use the thirty minutes before your daily break to organize your workspace, prepare lunches for the family, and do other tasks. Play your preferred music or podcast to enhance the effectiveness of this practice.
- Schedule some quiet time before bed to read, meditate, refocus, or do anything else that helps you sleep better.

Remember that developing routines into habits can take up to three months. Thus, be adaptable to the process and keep an eye on what's working and what needs to be changed. Realize that you can pick up the pieces and start over even if everything falls apart on a specific day.

How to Create Meaningful Rituals

While it's not necessary to ritualize every process, there are several that will help you perform at your best and provide value. It would help if you made rituals out of what matters most to you, but here are some ideas to get you started:

- Embrace thankfulness by making time every day to acknowledge the positive aspects of your life rather than dwelling solely on the negative. Gratitude can also be shown through thoughtful activities like prayer.

- Even if they have nothing to do with business, list your top priorities for the day on paper. This makes it easier to remember to prioritize specific habits, like working out or attending support groups.

- Get up earlier than you think you should. Even 30 minutes early can provide you the time you need for more critical introspective activities like journaling, yoga, gardening, running, etc.

Review some rituals that several CEOs, artists, and even previous presidents follow for amusement. Adhere to look after themselves, increase productivity, and encourage life advancement.

Making Wellbeing and Self-care a Priority

Nothing is more important than making time for your well-being. In contrast to antiquated notions, self-care is not selfish. It's an essential behavior that makes it easier for you to effectively show up for others, yourself, and your life.

Regarding taking care of oneself, the proverb "running on empty" is accurate. You can't help others if you aren't taking care of yourself first. So, how do we get better at it?

You may empower yourself and position yourself to live life to the fullest by establishing a foundation of good self-love and well-being behaviors through self-care activities.

What is self-care specifically?
Stress can be decreased, and pleasure and satisfaction can be increased by prioritizing your

well-being, a technique known as self-care. Self-care entails being aware of your emotions and making decisions—sometimes even sacrificing something—to protect your physical and emotional well-being.

Although face masks and mud baths are excellent self-care, self-care is much more than those decadent spa days and self-indulgent pampering sessions. Setting boundaries at work and scheduling necessary medical appointments are two ways to take care of yourself, even if they don't always feel enjoyable. Still, they're crucial for preserving one's physical, emotional, and mental well.

Recall that individual differences in self-care routines are acceptable. It all comes down to figuring out what makes you feel emotionally and physically refreshed.

What makes self-care crucial?

Self-care is crucial since it entails identifying and attending to your needs. Numerous aspects of your life can be improved by actively tending to your wellness.

1. Self-care could enhance physical well-being.
2. It can help you be kinder to yourself and boost your mental toughness.
3. It could elevate mood.
4. It could help chill you out and manage stress better.
5. Taking care of oneself could increase output.

How to draft a strategy for self-care

Making a self-care schedule helps you schedule time for activities that support your mental, emotional, and physical well-being. Because your needs may change over time, your self-care plan should likewise be flexible.

It's acceptable to review and modify your plan in response to your current state of mind. Recall that the purpose of a self-care plan is to replenish and revitalize yourself, not to add more things to your to-do list.

1. **Determine what kind of self-care would be most beneficial for you.**

Start by assessing your mental, emotional, and physical well-being. Making a meaningful self-care strategy starts with determining what needs to be addressed.

2. **Establish objectives**

What goals do you have for your self-care regimen? Establishing your goals will provide your self-care plan focus, whether it's stress reduction, better sleep, or just having more energy.

3. **Give your favorite self-care activities a top priority.**

List your favorite self-care activities based on your goals and self-evaluation. Exercise, meditation, quality time with loved ones, or engaging in a pastime could all be examples.

4. **Make a self-care routine that you can follow.**

Make time in your weekly or daily calendar for self-care tasks. These are non-negotiable appointments that you have with yourself.

5. **Monitor your development and modify your self-care schedule as necessary.**

Use an app or a basic diary to record your self-care routine and track your feelings. Modify your plan as necessary if something isn't working or if you find new beneficial activities.

Why Is Self-Care Your First Priority?

Most individuals today understand the significance of self-care, but they frequently put off taking steps to enhance their mental, emotional, and physical health. On the other hand, putting self-care first and forming self-empowering habits will improve your physical and psychological well-being and your sense of value and self-esteem. It will also help you appreciate yourself more and have a better self-image.

Additionally, it is a great way to strengthen your willpower and commitment to your goals, as well as your intrinsic motivation, which comes from within you independent of outside stimuli.

Naturally, it will also assist you in developing emotional self-control, recognizing and valuing your unique rhythms, and elevating your abilities to a new level. This is because practicing self-care will help you better understand who you are, identify your requirements, and establish new objectives for your development.

Prioritizing and concentrating on self-care teaches you to separate yourself from life experiences, which facilitates problem-solving psychologically, improves decision-making, and lowers the psychological risk factors associated with stress, anxiety, and depression. This does not make you immune to issues or psychiatric disorders; instead, it just means you will be more equipped to deal with them head-on and have more coping mechanisms.

Five (5) Useful Self-Care Strategies to Boost Your Wellness

Taking care of yourself doesn't mean sleeping in when you're exhausted or spending your free time doing something calming while you're depressed.

Respecting your body and mind and committing to your emotional stability and well-being—not as a duty but as an act of self-love—are all part of practicing self-care. It entails taking charge of your life, figuring out your basic requirements, and forming new routines that improve your emotional and physical well-being. Not sure where to begin?

Here are some fundamental self-care suggestions to enhance your well-being.

1. **Take Care of Your Nutrition:**

In addition to giving you more energy for everyday activities, a healthy, balanced diet helps control your body weight. It lowers your risk of developing several diseases like diabetes or cardiovascular disorders. But did you know that your mood is also influenced by the food you eat? The brain needs nourishment from food, much like other organs, to function. While some foods impede synaptic transmission between neurons, others enhance the release of specific neurotransmitters.

Consuming meals high in omega-3 fatty acids, like walnuts or sardines, and foods high in antioxidants, like berries, or B-group vitamins, like eggs, can help boost brain function and stimulate the mind. According to a recent study from Ohio State University, eating a healthy diet can often help lessen the symptoms of certain psychological disorders. The study found that eating a moderate amount of fruits and vegetables can help reduce the signs of hyperactivity and impulsivity in people with Attention Deficit Hyperactivity Disorder (ADHD). Furthermore, avoiding foods high in alcohol, hydrogenated fats, artificial sweeteners, or refined sugars are known to help prevent psychiatric illnesses like sadness and anxiety.

2. **Maintain Your Mental and Physical Activity:**

Living a physically and mentally active life is another essential self-care suggestion. It is beneficial to your musculoskeletal system, balance, mobility, coordination, and respiratory and cardiovascular systems to be physically active, especially outside. On the other hand, it significantly affects your mental health as well.

By encouraging the release of endorphins, being physically active promotes a positive sense of well-being and aids in relaxation, tension release, and stress reduction. Psychologists at the University of Vermont have demonstrated that it is an effective treatment for averting anxiety.

Maintaining mental activity is crucial at the same time. This helps delay or prevent issues like poor attention or illnesses like Alzheimer's by preventing cognitive decline and aging of brain processes. What mental exercises are there? Simple mental exercises like writing, reading, and listening to music might help you focus. Try word or number games, riddles, logic, and analytical games, or discover new topics to take things further.

3. Learn to Control Your Feelings:

Your emotions take control of you when you're unable to manage them. Thus, developing your emotional intelligence—a term made famous by American psychologist Daniel Goleman—refers to the capacity to identify and effectively control your emotions—is another crucial self-care recommendation. In addition to assisting you in developing empathy, addressing the root reasons for depression or lack of drive, and managing your anger and irritation more effectively, this skill will also help you reduce stress and anxiety and enhance your general sense of well-being.

To do this, you must develop self-awareness and learn to identify your emotions by setting aside little periods during the day to reflect on your feelings. It's time to learn how to control your emotions once you can identify them.

Do you need help to accomplish this? To quiet your feelings and take back control of them, try visualization, breathing exercises, or relaxation techniques. It's also a helpful strategy for managing tension and anxiety. Want to take things a bit further? Through cognitive restructuring—a potent approach that helps you replace negative thoughts with more positive ones to boost your mood—you can learn to create emotional distance from events and alter your understanding of them.

4. Embrace the Company of Value-Added Individuals:

Do you find it challenging to get together with friends? Do you work all day and rarely get to spend time with your family? Recall that building interpersonal ties is a crucial component of self-care. Having positive people in your life not only gives you the support you need when things get tough but also helps you fight loneliness, feel better about yourself, handle stress better, and, most importantly, feel better because physical contact raises serotonin and oxytocin levels. You can also exchange fresh experiences and develop your social skills.

Thus, consider again before returning a friend's invitation the next time. Plan activities with your family as well.

And close pals, ideally outdoors in nature. Furthermore, why not? Dare to mingle or strike up conversations with strangers you encounter. In addition to widening your social circle, meeting new people can inspire you to pursue interests outside your own and open your eyes to fresh perspectives on life.

5. Make Time for rest:

One further self-care practice you should start as soon as possible is setting aside time each day for relaxation. Sleep is vital for sustaining your energy levels for daily tasks. Sleeping for at least 8 hours a day aids in energy restoration, cell regeneration, and removing toxins that build up in the brain and cause diseases like Alzheimer's and cardiovascular issues. It also supports a more proactive mindset, better decision-making, and sustained focus.

But making time for relaxation is also crucial when it comes to self-care. You only need to practice mindful breathing for five minutes a day to reduce stress and anxiety, according to a Stanford University study by psychologists. Other options for de-stressing include dancing, going for a walk outdoors, or simply listening to music. You can even try meditation or relaxation techniques.

Lastly, remember that caring for yourself does not equate to selfishness. Self-love means putting your needs first and putting yourself before others. This not only enables you to take better care of those around you but also of yourself. It is, after all, difficult to assist people around you if you cannot take care of yourself."

Conclusion

Continual Growth

Growth is a crucial aspect of existence. This is clear to see. If our child, pet, or hair stopped growing, we would all be worried. That seems to suggest that something's not quite right.

Therefore, when we cease developing mentally, why is it so simple to neglect ourselves?

I believe that after we graduate from high school, we tend to stagnate and grow accustomed to our circumstances. This feeling comes from both experience and observation. Perhaps this is because we are no longer being forced or challenged to learn and grow through assignments and classes; alternatively, it might result from a hectic schedule, a lack of drive, or other difficulties.

For whatever reason, something stands in our way and keeps us from developing.
The absence of growth represents death. Nobody ever reaches adulthood. To cease developing is to pass away.

To progress further, we must aim for higher developmental stages. These new levels encompass spiritual growth, emotions, intellect, relationships, finances, and physical health.

Growing is the process of evolving throughout time. Growth, whether mental or physical, denotes motion within an object. And for the most part, growth is beneficial (except from The Force and disease). Physically, the wind, the water, and our bodies are in constant motion. It is essential to our life and is a natural occurrence.

Similarly, our existence and well-being depend just as much on mental development and transformation. Mental development helps you stay mentally alert, improves your performance at work, and gives you a sense of accomplishment and vigor.

For me, learning new things and improving at whatever I do are ongoing goals. I have to keep developing, learning, and understanding as a publisher.

I prefer to attempt to read something new every day for at least thirty minutes, think about it, and then write down what I've learned. This procedure forces me to comprehend what I've learned to the point that I can impart it to others. It is among the finest methods of learning, incidentally. It works similarly to how discussing an issue with someone else can help you figure it out.

What is the next stage of your life you would like to attain? In a year, where would you wish to be? Maybe this is your season of getting ready for something bigger. Everybody wants to improve their community, careers, and interpersonal connections.

We must be sincere about our growth and prepared to incur continuing costs. You have to be willing to take action to advance. Our ideas, objectives, aspirations, and wishes must be acted upon consciously. It is never too late to do the right thing, for the right reasons, in the right way.

So, where should we begin? Prioritize seeking God's kingdom and righteousness; all these things will follow. Make following God your top priority. Focusing on the wrong things causes most individuals to fail in life. Make God your top priority in life. You're going to move into a completely new realm. Step one and keep developing. Carry it out.

JASON M. TRAVER

Discover the Worlds Within My Books

Are you ready for a journey that will captivate your imagination, stir your emotions, and leave you craving more? Dive into my collection of books, where every page reveals new adventures, unforgettable characters, and stories that will stay with you long after you've turned the last page. Whether you're seeking heart-pounding thrillers, soul-stirring dramas, or fantastical realms, you'll find it here.

Grab your copy today and let the adventure begin!

Feel free to adjust based on your book genres or personal style! If you'd like to specify more details, like the book titles or themes, I can tailor it even further.

Thank You

www.ingramcontent.com/pod-product-compliance
Lightning Source LLC
Chambersburg PA
CBHW052240220526
45471CB00001B/130